(*continued from front flap*)

album and looking at them," Emmeline Garnett lets her readers relive with Newman some of the most significant events of his life: his acceptance at Oriel; the growth of the Oxford Movement; his soul-searching move toward Roman Catholicism; his ordination and later elevation to the cardinalate; his years at the Birmingham Oratory; his writing. This was a man whose spirituality so transcended all religious boundaries that a low-church minister who had been reading the cardinal's sermons wrote, shortly before Newman's death in 1890: "Surely it is right that I should tell you, if I could, how my life has been changed, how my spirit has been fashioned. . . ."

EMMELINE GARNETT, a Londoner, holds an Oxford University degree in English. She has been a teacher and is now a lecturer in a British training school. Miss Garnett is the author of *Florence Nightingale's Nuns* and *Charles de Foucauld* and has compiled *Seasons: A Cycle of Verse.*

D1269898

ARIEL BOOKS

Farrar, Straus & Giroux
19 Union Square West, New York 10003

Tormented Angel

Tormented
A Life of

ARIEL BOOKS

Angel
John Henry Newman

By Emmeline Garnett

Farrar, Straus & Giroux · New York

Contents

Tormented Angel

1

Requiem for a Cardinal

August 17, 1890

They are burying a Roman Catholic Cardinal in Birmingham.
The English are good at funerals, as they are good at any occasion that needs pomp and ceremony. They don't have a chance
like this once in twenty years, and they are making the most
of it.

What seems odd perhaps is that this grand funeral is
taking place in Birmingham, that red and black city of the
steely Midlands, dedicated to the hard and practical things of
life. There have been one or two voices raised to suggest that
John Henry Newman, being not of an age but for all time,
should be buried in Westminster Abbey, where the nation's
heroes go. But the idea has come to nothing, and he is being
buried in Birmingham, which is the only home he has known
for over forty years.

There would only be one other possible graveyard for
him—Oxford. If the Roman Catholic Church did not refuse
cremation at this time, he might have been cremated. And
then where would you have scattered his ashes? In Trinity

College, Oxford, which started him on his bright scholar's career? Or Oriel College, where his genius came to flower? A little pinch would have to go, perhaps, under the pulpit of the University Church, where, if you have ears to hear, his silver-tongued ghost must still hold enthralled a shadowy congregation. Or up at Littlemore, where he was for a short time happy.

But after all it is Birmingham, and a final contrast in a life full of contrasts—the smoky surroundings and the pale scholar; the city given up to practical things, and the man who cared less for practical things than almost anyone else one could find within a hundred miles.

"The thing about J.H.N.," as someone said later, "was that he just didn't give a damn for this world at all."

Well, this world, which in the past has given a great many damns for him, has turned out in strength to see the last of John Henry Newman, Cardinal.

They have turned up in thousands. The railway stations have swarmed with arrivals in special first-class trains, one more important than the last, so that the poor stationmasters are giddy with bowing from side to side. The hotels are full of black coats and purple. Birmingham has never in its life seen so many reverend gentlemen at once.

The Oratory Church is draped from top to bottom in black with gold fringes. The pulpit is all but hidden under an immense respectful black drapery embroidered with the Cardinal's coat of arms. *Cor ad cor loquitur* is the motto: "Heart speaks to heart." And it's quite true. In all those crowds in the streets outside—at least twenty thousand people, behind the broad blue backs of the policemen, stand to see the procession go by—it would be instructive if you could look behind the faces and see how many are not standing there just out of idle curiosity, though that plays its part too, but because they have a real feeling of having lost somebody, something, out of their lives.

Instructive, because it is largely a Protestant crowd, and this is a prince of the Roman Church. And Catholicism is still not entirely respectable. It is still very possible at this date to raise an easy hate by saying "papist," as at a future time it will be by saying "Communist." Things are improving, though. People are beginning to accept that one can be a papist and at the same time a good and honorable man—not necessarily a scoundrel, an Irishman, a bloody foreigner, a spy, a hypocrite, or a fool. That it is so is largely the result of one man's life, the man they are burying this afternoon. It is for him, and him alone, that the Mayor and the Corporation of Birmingham are even now struggling into their furred gowns and civic gold chains, in order to attend, in full marching order, a Roman ceremony in a Roman church.

"Our English Christianity is something different from what it would have been, had he never lived." A Canon of Westminster Abbey says this from his Protestant pulpit.

"One could not think of Newman, and think of Catholicism as all tawdriness." That is the powerful voice of the London *Times*.

Some enthusiastic newspaper clipper counted 170 notices of Newman's death in journals of all sorts, right down to the sporting papers such as *Rod and Gun*. Most of them—not all, but most—are friendly.

Of course, they have not all come to the funeral. The days of widespread press coverage are still a long way off. Anyway, there wouldn't be room. The church, packed as tight as it will go, does not hold more than four hundred, and some of them can hardly breathe. However, in odd corners here and there, behind pillars, there are reporters from the big papers, trying to scribble notes without making their shorthand pads too obvious, and it is from them that we know most of what happens on this day.

The church is always rather gloomy. Now that it is wrapped in black, the solemn and ornate trimmings of a nineteenth-century funeral, there is hardly any light at all, except where the candles shine.

From very early morning the little bells have been tinkling almost continuously, as lines of visiting priests and bishops murmur their Masses at the side altars. Each one hurries through the brief black Mass as fast as reverence permits, and makes way for the next. But this slight busy scurrying around the edges of the church makes no difference to the stillness at the center.

In front of the main altar, surrounded by a hedge of lighted candles, the body of John Henry Newman lies in state. Robed in his full splendor of scarlet and crimson, with miter, gloves, crozier, the small shrunk figure seems almost lost. Over him, a deep purple pall with a gold cross, and lying on that, the cardinal's red hat with its enormous ropes and tassels, that strange, unwearable symbol of power.

People pass, and look. Many of them pray. The crowds have been coming in curiosity, in affection, in respect, ever since Monday, to stop for a minute and look at that remote waxen face, all nose and chin. ("Oo, *Punch!*" said a little girl.)

Their thoughts were no doubt as mixed as the comments of the newspapers.

"A man who walked with God," said the *Christian World*.

"Cardinal Newman's ecclesiastical career has been a blight and an evil, rather than a blessing to the nation," said the *English Churchman*.

"A mighty man has fallen, yet we are much as we were," remarked the *Times*, which rarely commits itself.

But the *Record* reporter, with warmth and understanding, burst out: "If the Church of England could not keep Newman . . . the Church of Rome could not use him. . . . The Church of Rome has had such men in her fold before. It sometimes canonizes them when they are dead, but it never trusts them when they are alive."

A perceptive remark, which might have been taken to heart by some of the hundreds of sober-suited mourners who are waiting in church for the funeral service to begin. Two dukes at least, a fair scattering of princes, all the Catholic nobility and gentry. Many of them, even those with gray hair and a touch of rheumatism, have known Newman as a famous man all their lives. When they were inky schoolboys, his name was a household word, so long has his life been, bridging a whole century. 1801: he was born, only just missing the eighteenth century. 1890: he is dead, and we are in spitting distance of the twentieth.

Now four hundred voices rise and fall to that most majestic Latin hymn, the *Dies Irae*. Plain chant from so many throats cannot fail to move. At the last verse the tapers are lighted, each man passing on the flame to his neighbor, flickering from person to person until the whole church glows. The small flames shine upward on people's faces. In the front row, where seventeen bishops sit in purple and lace, you can see that some of these old men are moved with a deep sense of loss. Some are concealing behind a churchmanlike façade a sigh of relief that "the most dangerous man in England" is finally, safely at rest. Once he is underground, they can afford to praise him, just a little, cautiously. Some will not even dare to do so much.

You might think they would have felt safe for the last ten years. Surely the old lion's teeth were drawn long ago, the old man a recluse in saintly crimson with a sweet smile. But bishops know better, for ideas are catching, particularly this man's ideas. A room with a candle in it can never be the same as a room without; so England with Newman alive, however low the wick seemed to sink, was one place, and with Newman dead, another. The danger is, of course, that his ideas may continue to glow even when he has been tucked into his narrow bed in the Oratory graveyard, where the yellow St.-John's-wort spreads like a weed through the grass. That is a danger they will have to guard against.

Bishop Clifford of Clifton goes up into the pulpit to preach the sermon. Although he is the oldest bishop present, he served John Henry Newman's first Mass in Rome, forty-five years ago, when he was a young student and the great man was already middle-aged, with half his life's work behind him.

The old bishop spoils his peroration by breaking down in the middle, swallows and blows his nose before he can carry on. He has always been a faithful friend, when they were few enough. "The Church of Rome has had such men in her fold before. It sometimes canonizes them when they are dead, but it never trusts them when they are alive." It would not do to preach from a text like that, but Clifford must feel like doing so. Instead he rejoices, with generous exaggeration, in his old friend's personal gifts: "his kind and gentle manner . . . his patience and sympathy . . . knowing how to bear with the weaknesses of others . . . and how to handle, not only the minds, but the hearts of men."

Without doubt, to some men John Henry Newman was like that. It is perhaps the mark of a very great man that he arouses completely contradictory reactions in different people. Bishop Clifford, the good old man, is not the only person to emphasize one side of Newman to the exclusion of others. In the foreseeable future, people will go on doing just that. Hundreds of millions of words will pour off the printing presses of the world to prove that there are as many different pictures of him as there are different people writing them. He has roused strong feelings while he was alive. The feelings will not be any less strong seventy-five years after his funeral, or, perhaps, a hundred and seventy-five years after. It will take more than a century to fathom his character.

We feel the strange attraction now, and they felt it then. Twenty thousand people were not in the streets on a wet day out of curiosity only. The church emptied, the swaying coffin was loaded on to the hearse, the procession moved off to Rednal Green, followed by a winding string of carriages, all black, black-horsed, with the blinds drawn down. (The convenience of this was that no one could see whether there was anyone inside or not. You could show respect by sending your carriage to a funeral without actually having to go yourself.) The tireless newspaper reporters darted about in the crowd with their pencils poised. Any story was good enough to report, and everybody had a story. Even the cripple who swept the crossing outside the "Plough and Harrow," and who once got sixpence from His Eminence, ten years ago, says so, and is sure of getting into print.

That Sunday, while the flowers are still fresh on his grave, the life of John Henry Newman was the subject of sermons from thousands of pulpits up and down the country. Naturally, in Catholic churches—but hundreds of Protestant clergymen also spoke of him, kindly, reverently, sadly. Though many of them may have had to register their feeling that his conversion or perversion to Roman Catholicism was the one terrible blot on his life, still they generously acknowledged his scholarship, his leadership, his greatness. Then they led their congregations in singing "Lead, kindly light," and the church-warden lowered the flag of St. George on the tower to half-mast.

But where does the secret lie? Why did so many people think and feel that they had lost a great man? What is a "great" man?

"We are baffled," says one of his biographers, "when we try to attach a label to him and to assign him to a neat and precise category. Let it be granted that he was not a theologian, nor a philosopher, nor a historian, nor a preacher, nor a poet, at least not in the front rank."[1]

And yet, if he was not any of those, "at least in the front rank," what on earth was he? For those were the only areas of life in which he declared any interest. Much else, much that was very important, was a completely closed book to him. In all the multitudinous writings, in the volumes upon volumes of letters, where biographers burrow like enthusiastic moles, there is no mention of social problems that turned the nine-

[1] Autobiographical writings of J. H. N., ed. Henry Tristram (New York: Sheed & Ward).

teenth century into a bear garden, no mention of its wars, its explorations, its politics, its discoveries, hardly any note of its art, literature, music, daily affairs.

Well, this short book is not going to try to fill any gaps. We are going to do no more than skate over the surface of that life, looking at some of the things that happened to him, some of the things that he made happen. We will sort out a few old snapshots, and paste them into an album, and look at them. At the end, one may be just as ignorant of the deep springs inside this extraordinary person, but one cannot help being impressed and moved, as once people were moved when he came into the room, although they could not explain why, or what it was.

When Newman was made a Cardinal, one of his old friends was already Lord Chief Justice—not, you would say, a person to be lightly overawed by any living man.

"I cannot analyze it or explain it, but to this hour he interests and awes me like no other man I ever saw. He is as simple and humble and playful as a child, and, yet, I am with a being unlike anyone else. He lifts me up for a time and subdues me—if I said frightens me it would hardly be too strong."

It is time to travel backward from the end of his life to the beginning, across the stretch of a century, to see what clues we can pick up along the road. It may be that we shall end by saying with another of the many writers who have tried to tackle this intractable subject:

"As for JHN, though he sometimes provokes an exasperated sigh or an ironic chuckle, who can do other than revere that brave, kind, solitary, gifted, tormented angel?"[2]

[2] Sean O'Faolain: *Newman's Way* (New York: Devin-Adair; 1952).

2

Home for the Holidays

June 6, 1810

We know the date exactly, because of the letter. June 6, 1810.
And the scene is Dr. Nicholas's School for the Sons of Gentlemen at Ealing, which is now an undistinguished suburb of
London but was then a large village quite outside the city. At
Dr. Nicholas's School, the sons of gentlemen between the ages
of seven and nineteen were well instructed and tolerably
happy. The Doctor was a civilized man, and under his care
the boys, too, were civilized, at least as civilized as 250 boys in
crowded conditions can ever hope to be. The food was not
bad; there was no more measles, scarlet fever, or ringworm
than could be expected; the standards of classical study were
not quite up to those of Eton or Winchester, but then neither
were the standards of brutality. In summer especially, since
the school stood in twelve acres of its own land, and the bathing places of the river Thames were only a mile away, there
were far worse places in which to scramble into a little education than Dr. Nicholas's School.

On Wednesday afternoons the writing master paid a

visit, and on Wednesday, June 6, the sounds and smells of hot summer drifted in through the window of a great bare, chalky classroom, over fifty or sixty bent heads, fifty or sixty pens scratching, squeaking, spluttering across the paper.

"Your best, your *very best* copperplate today, young gentlemen, please. Remember, light on the upstrokes, heavy on the down. Remember the happy occasion, and let us have elegance in every word."

In some such way the writing master must have encouraged his large class, which, for once, was concentrating fiercely, though every now and again a head was turned sideways to wink and grin at a neighbor, while over all there rose a thin, contented humming, like a hive of good bees with honey in store. The Lower School was writing home.

June 6, 1810

Dear Mama,

I have again the pleasure to announce the approach of our vacation. It begins as usual on the 21st instant when I hope to see you as well as it leaves,

Dear Mama,

Your dutiful son.

Among the others, and quicker than most of them, John Henry Newman signed his name in full with a happy flourish and handed in his letter to be passed fit for posting.

A beaky, solemn nine-year-old, still young enough to wear a pie-frill collar above a short round jacket with two rows of buttons, he was already an experienced schoolboy. This was his fifth vacation letter and he knew the wording by heart. Already five half-years at boarding school! His parents, very proud of their clever eldest child, and with plenty more crowding the nursery, had pushed him ahead and sent him off to school when he was not much over seven. Even then, he had carried with him a weight of things already learned.

He could read perfectly well when he was five, not only print but handwriting, for at that age his father sent him a letter which said:

"You will observe that you must learn something new every day, or you will no longer be called a clever boy. I, therefore, hope that by next Thursday you will have got your Multiplication Table by heart and have also begun to learn your Pence Table. I mean to examine you as to your Multiplication Table, and if I find you improve I intend after a time to buy a nice Copy Book and teach you to write."

John Henry responded to this sort of encouragement, with the result that at nine he was going fast up the school— too fast, some of the other boys thought bitterly, as he piped up with the right answer time and again, shooting past the eleven- and twelve-year-olds to the top of his class. The masters liked him: schoolmasters do tend to like a boy who would rather read Rollins's *Ancient History* than play at tipcat or marbles. Especially when the boy has ideas of his own, and speaks them.

Even the great Dr. Nicholas himself cocked a friendly eye in the direction of John Newman. When John was found listening outside the drawing-room door to the music on one of the Doctor's "musical evenings," he was not sent up to the dormitory with a flea in his ear.

"What, do you like it?" said Dr. Nicholas cheerfully. "Come in and sit down."

He was a quiet, serious child who could be trusted not to disturb the adults. He kept a diary and wrote in it every day,

entries that were brief and to the point. "Flew kite" . . . "Had
chicken pocks" . . . "Dancing" . . . "Rained". . .

Already, on that summer day when he wrote the letter
home, it was a fortnight since he had been able to enter in his
diary, with triumph: "Got into Ovid and Greek." That he was
already "into Greek" was something to take home with his
end-of-term report. His father would be pleased. His mother
would be pleased, which mattered more. And the nursery
crowd would be impressed according to their ages and understanding. Charlie was eight, Harriet seven, Frank five, and
Jemima two. Mary, who was six months old, would not be
impressed, but he would tell her about it all the same, and
she would chuckle at him toothlessly. John was very fond of
that baby. He was indeed very fond of all his family, though
he was too reserved to show much affection. This was not surprising, considering the impressionable years spent away from
home, months at a time in the hard, bracing, tough, crowded
conditions of schoolroom and dormitory. It is more surprising
that any of the homely feelings remained green at all. But
they did—after a fashion. Not perhaps in words, but there are
other ways of showing things. There was the incident, for
instance, of the netting box.

This had happened in the previous holidays, when John
was not yet nine. He had come home in December from his
half year at school with a plan in mind. He was going to buy
his Mama a netting box, and it was already quite noticeable
that what John decided to do got done.

For a long time (at least a year, almost forever in the
children's minds), Mrs. Newman had been netting a fine veil
as what she called her "five minutes' work." This had to be
something light and elegant that could be picked up and put

down whenever there was a moment. (It was so easy for middle-class women to be totally idle that the conscientious ones
had to plan seriously how not to slip into this condition.) Mrs.
Newman kept her veil, and the balls of white thread, the gold
thimble (her best one), and the little bright steel scissors, near
her always.

Perhaps this nearness made John think of the box. It was
something which was sure to stay close by his mother while he
was away. There was so much going away, and always, it
seemed, a new baby to take up her time when he came back
again. Whatever the reason, the idea of the netting box took
firm hold.

He counted up his money. A shilling or two left over
from school, which was unusual: he must have been saving,
for he usually came back quite cleaned out. A half sovereign
from a visiting uncle who had felt a touch of the Christmas
spirit. A five-shilling piece from a little collection of odd coins
that his mother kept for him—it was a curiosity rather than an
antique, so it seemed all right to take it out and spend it in a
good cause. And then his weekly allowance, what the children
called their "pay," which his father would not hand over until
the last day of the holidays, but he could borrow from Aunt
Betsy on the strength of it. Totted up on a scrap of paper, all
this came to an impressive sum.

But even with the money in his pocket, it was not all that
easy to buy the box.

Mr. Newman was a prosperous banker and had a town
house and a country house, one for winter and one for summer. None of the children liked the London house, where
they spent the winter months. It was high and narrow and
dark, and the children were penned in top-floor nurseries, not

allowed to go out alone, except perhaps into the garden of the
square, where they could play in safety behind iron railings.
The streets were dirty and dangerous places where child steal-
ing was still fairly common; they were forbidden territory
unless one was in the grip of a grown-up hand, and sometimes
one could fret for days waiting before an escort could be
found. Life was organized for adults, not children; the nurses
were busy with the babies, and the middle years of childhood
could be very boring.

To buy his netting box, John had to wait until Aunt
Betsy, the only adult who was in on the secret, could take him
out shopping. The first day, she was busy—that was Friday.
On Saturday they were on the verge of going out, when it
rained—it takes an effort of mind to understand how important the weather could be in those days before raincoats
and rubber boots. The third day was Sunday. The fourth day
was interrupted by a gaggle of lady visitors paying a morning
call. John Henry was a severely self-controlled boy, but he
was brought near to tears of frustration.

In the end the box was bought and given to his mother,
and the occasion was most satisfactory. The other children
were stupefied with admiration. There was something so
grandly casual about John's buying Mama a present that had
cost more than a sovereign. They gathered around, stroking
and fingering. Harriet, aged seven, remembered every detail
of that box to the end of her life.

"Its form was rather oblong and sloped off at the top. It
was made of the root of the yew tree and seemed spangled all
over with polished shaded stars, covered, as they were, with
fibres of the most delicate stencilling. It stood upon four softly
shining, smooth, enduring balls of ivory, of the purest white.

It was lined with bright red, with red velvet cushions, and in one of the well-contrived compartments within lay, in tempting readiness, the brightest of keys."

In other words, it was not just what some nine-year-olds might be deceived into thinking was a beautiful box: it really was beautiful. And the choice had not been made by chance either. John had turned the shop upside down to find the box that satisfied him.

His mother, of course, was delighted, and from then on the box went with her everywhere. It even went to the seaside. For the first time that summer, in the holidays that were heralded by John's letter from school, the whole family packed up and went to the sea, all except the baby, who was sent off with her nursemaid to stay with Grandma.

It was just beginning to be the right thing for a successful man like John Newman to do, to take his family on the expensive journey down to the south coast. Sixty miles took two days to accomplish, the large family in two chaises, changing horses every ten miles, and spending the night in an inn. The servants and the heavy luggage followed more slowly by coach.

The children had a great time that summer. Father took them bathing, and out in a rowboat; they rode on donkeys; they played on the sand; they scrambled on the rocks. Sometimes, especially when visiting uncles had been in a generous mood, they went down to the toyshop and spent a happy afternoon discussing what to buy.

Harriet remembered a day when John and Charlie spent hours trying out swords and drums, while she sat perched on a high stool, waiting for the boys to finish their shopping so they could all get on with their walk on the sand.

"Doesn't this little girl get anything?" asked a lady who came into the shop.

"No, thank you," said Harriet primly. "It isn't my turn."

The lady, who knew nothing about large families, was touched by what she regarded as exceptional unselfishness, and insisted on buying Harriet a pretty pencil box as a reward. Harriet was grateful but surprised, for even in the nursery they were a very disciplined family, and taking turns came naturally.

It was John who led the tightly knit group and gave it its color. They drew together in the face of strangers and did not much welcome other children, playing best alone, and John thought this was as it should be. "Oh, *him*," he once said disparagingly of young Frank, "he likes *every*body."

Harriet remembered other incidents that showed the shape of John's character. When he and Charlie climbed the Hastings cliffs that summer by the sea, and nearly got stuck, Charlie panicked. John kept his head and came down the narrow sheep track with complete self-control.

An even more John-like episode must have happened the year before, at their country cottage at Norwood. Three-year-old Frank fell off the Shetland pony and the gardener carried him indoors half-conscious, and Mrs. Newman fainted. John withdrew quietly to the dining room and mixed not one but two different glasses of wine and water so that she could take whichever she fancied. When he got back, a glass in each hand, he found he could not get at his mother through the screen of twittering aunts and nursemaids. So he laid the two glasses down where they would be handy, and went off to his room, inwardly shaken but expecting nobody to console *him*. He was eight years old, the eldest, utterly reliable John.

As compensation for this outer shell of control, the inside of his head churned with strange fancies. When for the moment there was nothing much to interest him in the outside world, he could withdraw within himself, so far within that he sometimes seemed to lose touch with ordinary things and take off into a world of Arabian Nights, full of magic. Suppose there were no such thing as living, that all this were a dream, this apparently solid world, what would happen when he woke up? Suppose he were not a real person at all, but some sort of spirit, or angel, what then?

If he disliked going back to school when the six weeks' midsummer break was over, we may presume that he never showed it. The lovely seaside trip was over, but it was only the beginning of August. Although John, and perhaps this time Charlie too, had to go back to school at Ealing, the rest of the family did not go back to the London house but to the cottage at Norwood, which was their summer place. Like Ealing, it is swallowed up in London now, but then it was a country of woods and hills to the south of the city, with very few houses. If the pony jumped the paddock fence, which it sometimes did in a willful moment, it might be a week before they got it back.

The Norwood cottage was the children's idea of heaven. Here they had real freedom to run and ride and play, to be brown and noisy and not afraid of disturbing anybody. They had much more of their mother's company too, for the cottage was too small for segregation. Harriet used to gaze at the funny little house, with its window eyes on each side of a front-door nose, and consider what a kind friendly face it had and how, when she grew up, she would like to have just such an expression.

It was November 1 before they migrated back to town that year, already more than halfway through the boys' school term and only six weeks before the Christmas holiday. The Ealing boys had already made themselves wooden calendars, with notches for the days, which were struck off one by one with a penknife.

And then a sad thing happened on the very day that Mrs. Newman went up to London to open up the house that had been closed all summer, the children getting ready to follow from Norwood the next day.

A suspicious-looking character got into the drawing room while she was out. Ann the housemaid let him in, and stayed to keep an eye on him; she didn't trust anybody who was so obviously not a gentleman. He tried to get rid of her, pretending to write a note to Mrs. Newman, but Ann hovered, shaking up the curtains, straightening the soft cushions, freshening the fire, anything to keep him in sight.

Unluckily, at that moment the baker rang the doorbell down below, and rang, and rang. Ann was torn between leaving the stranger alone for a few moments and letting the family come home that evening to a breadless house. In the end she went down to the baker, and the stranger, thinking, it seemed, that he had found a valuable jewel case, slipped Mrs. Newman's netting box under his coat and left.

It was never seen again. They heard that a local pawnbroker had offered two shillings to the thief. ("*Two* shillings." The nursery throbbed with indignation. "Only two shillings for John's beautiful box with Mama's nearly finished veil inside it, and the scissors!") But the thief had also thought two shillings too little and had gone off with the box, presumably to some other pawnbroker farther away.

Mrs. Newman wrote straightaway to John at Ealing, telling him of the loss, and back by return came the answer, grandly penned in John Henry's best style, which was always flowery.

"Vex not yourself, dearest Mama, over the loss of a trifling box" . . . wrote John Henry Newman from the maturity of his nine and a half years. Inside the letter was another note marked, "For Aunt Betsy *alone*," and this said, more childishly, "I shall buy Mama another box."

And he did. The children never liked it so well. For them it was just a box, without the astonishing elegance of the first one. It was probably by now less impressive that John should go to grand stores and buy his mother expensive gifts. Mrs. Newman, though, liked it better. The effort involved in buying one box was remarkable. To follow it with a replacement was even more remarkable. But it was all of a piece with what she felt about her eldest son. He was cut out to be the eldest, the reliable, the sensible, the intelligent, the controlled, the one who, whatever happened, would see to things. "I have no fear," was his mother's favorite remark. "John will manage."

Note: Most of the material for this chapter, especially the story of the netting box, is taken from Harriet's book of stories called *Family Adventures*. There is no way of proving that these are true stories, but they sound like it.

3

A Trinity Man

June 11, 1817

Another summer day, this time in Oxford, and the city's stone walls echoing to the clatter of Commemoration festivities to mark the end of the academic year. It was the one occasion when the solemn old bachelor city flowered into gaiety. All day a thousand gowns and tasseled mortarboards paraded the cobbled streets and the shady river walks, escorting ladies in muslins and ribbons: the long midsummer evenings were gay with the sound of music and dancing from open windows.

The scene was more picturesque because the statute had recently been enforced which made it an offense for an undergraduate to be seen within the city except in his cap and gown. If a man wanted to walk or ride in the country in more ordinary gear, he had first to skulk through the Oxford streets, avoiding the proctors. Not till he had crossed Magdalen or Folly Bridge was he safe from being picked up and punished for the misdemeanor of being improperly dressed.

This was a tedious regulation, irksome to all young men, except perhaps a freshman in his first glow of self-importance.

On this occasion, June 11, 1817, John Henry Newman, aged all of sixteen and four months, could hardly wait to get into the uniform that within a few months he would probably long to discard.

You have to peer closely to see him in this picture of high-summer Oxford, for he is in the depths of one of Oxford's many tailors' shops, which flourished on the vanity of young men with money, and sometimes went bankrupt on the vanity of young men without money. At this time it was altogether too easy and fashionable to run up enormous bills. Not that John Henry Newman is about to run up bills. The smallish allowance from his father will be scrupulously laid out on necessities, and he is unlikely to be extravagant. Just possibly he may spend more than he can afford on books or music, but not on clothes.

All the same, this is his first day in Oxford, and he has rushed to the tailor's shop the instant his father, who delivered him by post chaise to the Promised Land, left for home. And here he is. Behind the diamonded windowpanes, where the tailor's assistants sit sewing cross-legged to catch the best of the daylight, inside past the bales of cloth and worsted, and rolls of silk, right at the back of the dark shop, in front of a long mirror, he is being fitted for an academic gown by a tailor who hands him into it, pats it and smoothes it, with the solemn joy of a man gazing on a work of art. (He knows how to recognize freshmen, and flatter them, this tailor.) He sidles and wheedles, looks over his customer's shoulder with his head to one side, flicks a speck of dust from the shoulder, tweaks a fold.

"I could make you one, sir, I could make you twenty, but you wouldn't get a better fit, not if I was to sit at it till Sunday. Beautiful, sir, beautiful."

In the depths of the greenish mirror John could see himself—big sharp nose, shortsighted brown eyes screwing up to see better, hair that would not stay combed but flapped over his forehead, lanky boyish figure, all transformed by the black classical folds of the gown that he did not want to take off now that he had it on, as the tailor very well knew.

"To be sure, I could shorten it a trifle for you if you insist, sir, but you may well grow taller. Gentlemen usually do . . ."

It ended as they had both foreseen, with John shrugging into it as though he had been wearing a gown all his life, settling the cap on his head at what he hoped was the right angle, and stepping out into the sunshiny streets, in great glory, on his way back to his newly possessed rooms at Trinity College. *Home*, he thought, exhilarated, *home*, in an Oxford college. He had dreamed of it so long, and now it had happened. Already the porter at the gate recognized him. He crossed the quadrangle, climbed his staircase, shut the door of his rooms, and sat down to consider and to start a letter home. Someone had to share the almost choking sense of achievement.

There were particular reasons why, young as he was, he should settle down with a great longing for security into the quiet niche of his first college rooms.

This time a year past, he had been at the top of Dr. Nicholas's School, the quickest scholar they had ever had, a clever, bookish, gentle boy who lorded it over his sisters, alternately quarreled and conspired with the brothers who challenged his leadership, loved his father and silently adored his mother.

He was just about to leave school when his world crashed. His father's bank stopped payment. For a while,

things were too uncertain for John to leave school. Kind Dr.
Nicholas reassured them about the fees ("When it suits, my
dear Mr. Newman, when it suits") and kept the boys during
the subsequent turmoil. The girls were packed off to Grandma's at Norwood, and Mrs. Newman directed all her energies
to helping her husband. He needed her help. The failure
broke him. Although it was not immediately apparent, his
head for business and his confidence had both gone, he was
vague and touchy, and his relations with his children deterio-
rated. In the days when a father's authority was exalted so
high within the family circle, it must have been very difficult
for him to climb down from his pedestal and admit that he
had made a mess of things. The strain, at any rate, was too
great for Mr. Newman. He became a rather shadowy, miserable, querulous figure, and he died seven years later, com-
paratively young but unable any longer to cope.

Among other burdens, he may well have felt jealous of
his eldest son; in everything that mattered, they leaned more
and more heavily on John. John would arrange things, his
mother said. John would advise on the girls' lessons and on his
brothers' future. John could be counted on to *manage*.

It was no wonder that, even if we are too kind to call him
a prig, John was much too solemn for his age. In his fifteenth
summer, under the double influence of a long and tedious
fever that he endured alone in the sickroom at school, and the
friendship of an extremely religious schoolmaster, a Mr. May-
ers, John underwent a religious conversion that shook him to
his foundations and set the pattern for the rest of his life, so
that looking back in old age, he said: "It is difficult to realize
or imagine the identity of the boy before and after August
1816. . . . I can look back at the end of seventy years as if on

another person." We have to leave it there, under the decent veil he himself drew in these ambiguous words. We don't know, and can't find out, exactly what happened. Something violent, from his own estimate: "Thy wonderful grace turned me right around, when I was more like a devil than a wicked boy. . . ." Pious exaggeration? Or a vision of the really alarming possibilities of evil inside himself? The curtain stays drawn.

The eventful year ended with his entrance at Trinity College, Oxford. Money was not yet as scarce as all that. Mr. Newman could still afford to pay for his son's education. It all seems delightfully casual: a post chaise at the door, the driver saying, "Where to, sir?" and Mr. Newman pondering. Should they start for Oxford or Cambridge? And John standing by with his portmanteau packed, apparently unconcerned which university it was to be, so long as he arrived at one of them.

It was Oxford in the end, and at Oxford it was Trinity College, which had no vacancy at the time but would have one in the summer. This six-months delay was not a bad thing. Oxford proved to be tough enough for a boy of sixteen; if he had gone into residence six months earlier, it would have been that much worse.

And now here he was, John Henry Newman, sitting in his own rooms, not the grandest set of rooms in college, but even so with a generous sense of space and privacy: a good sitting room, a small bedroom, a tiny pantry, and, best invention of all, double doors. The first one served the ordinary purposes of a door, but the outer one, the *oak,* insured absolute privacy. When that was closed, by old tradition no one dared knock, and no one could enter.

It was just the place for a scholarly sensitive boy, all of whose adventures had happened, and would happen, within

his own mind. Here he found himself in a stronghold that for
seven hundred years had been dedicated, though not always
successfully, to things of the mind. This was his world.

John went to his window and looked out on a landscape
of ancient gray walls. Trinity was newly conditioned, com-
paratively speaking, as it had been largely rebuilt only a hundred years before, but the walls were crumbling, as the soft
Oxford stone always crumbles, giving a strong foothold to
plants and mosses. That June day, the walls he could see from
his window were covered with dark red snapdragons; tough,
wiry little plants, their roots sink into the very stuff of the
walls, and to pull them out you have to tear the plant to
pieces. John said to himself, "I shall stay here till I die. This is
home to me now."

A knock on the door announced his first visitor. Another
undergraduate, John Bowden, had been sent by his tutor to
look after young Newman and see that he got down to five
o'clock dinner in Hall. The two Johns took to each other at
once. They found that they shared a birthday, on February
21, though Bowden was nineteen to Newman's sixteen. As
they went down to Hall, the two seem to have struck up an
instant pact, a godsend to John Newman, who was not good
at quick and casual friendship. From that time on they were
inseparable, reading together, eating together, walking and
boating together. Their characters seemed to fit like the two
halves of a walnut.

The first dinner, the first introduction to corporate college life, was a fascinating meal. A multitude of dishes was
spread carelessly on tables so large and so old that they seemed
to be the forest itself lying prone and polished. The food was
both good and plentiful—wastefully so, to anyone brought up

to a careful family dinner, where the leg of mutton went the round of the table and then out to the kitchen to do for the servants. Here the tables were jammed with dishes—legs of mutton, whole pink salmon, chickens roasted and boiled, gooseberry, raspberry, apricot pies. Of course, it was Commemoration Week, which may have had something to do with it. Everyone sat where he liked and took what he liked from any dish near him. The strangest thing of all was the plate: ancient battered crested pewter and lopsided pottery which seemed to have been in constant service since the college was built four hundred years before.

Next day the numbers were considerably thinner, and thereafter they grew less and less, until John Newman was left almost alone in college. It was what they called Little Trinity term, only three weeks long, before the long vacation. The young freshman was obliged to stay the full three weeks, but most others left immediately after Commemoration, unless they were hard-reading men, and Trinity had few of those. Even Bowden rode off to the country.

On the whole, it was a lonely and frustrating three weeks. All John wanted, now that he had arrived in Oxford, was someone who would help him get down to work, and this proved astonishingly difficult to find. Nobody seemed interested, nobody would give him a reading list for the coming vacation, lectures were long finished. If it was true, as Bowden had said, that Mr. Short, the Trinity tutor, was stricter, harder-working, and therefore less popular than his predecessor, it was hard to believe. Certainly he had had the kindness to see that the lonely schoolboy was looked after on his first day in college, but he did nothing at all about John's thirst for work. "Don't worry, plenty of time, wait till you come up in

the Michaelmas term," seems to have been his theme. But
John had already spent six months hanging about, idleness
was no pleasure to him then or ever, and he was at the brightest pitch of his young intellectual powers. He wanted to be
stretched. No one stretched him. He read all alone in his
rooms, his eyes hurt, and he was miserable.

Some bright spark invited him to a party, but this was not
a success. Going to bed drunk was still the one-way ticket to
manhood for many adolescents, but John Newman, prickly
with courage, priggishness, and obstinacy, withdrew in disgust and went to bed early instead.

Presumably during the afternoons he wandered about
that beautiful city, up the great curve of the High Street,
called the finest street in Europe, in and out of medieval
churches and colleges. He must have explored the Bodleian
Library, with its 300,000 books, more than any other library
except the Vatican. "There is shewn," says a guidebook published the same year, "the original warrant for the execution
of King Charles I, and Queen Elizabeth's missal or prayer-
book, fully illuminated."

Perhaps he crossed from the Bodleian to the Museum,
and saw among other treasures "a large magnet of oval shape,
18 inches long, twelve wide, and which supports a weight of
145 pounds . . . a very curious model of a ship; a picture
of our blessed Saviour going to his crucifixion, composed
of humming bird feathers . . . and many other curiosities of
nature and art, too numerous to mention."

But no number of curiosities of nature and art could well
fill in the empty hours before he walked back across Broad
Street to dine in the hall at Trinity.

"I am at the head of the table at dinner," he wrote home,

"because I am the only one; at least I sometimes nearly finish my dinner before the remaining few drop in. The other day I had a nice dinner set before me of veal cutlets and peas so much to myself that I could hear the noise I made chewing thro' the empty hall; till at length one came in and sat opposite to me, but I had not been introduced to him, and he could not speak to me. Consequently we preserved an amicable silence, and conversed with our teeth."

It was not a very good start to his Oxford life, but John did not let it color his opinions of the university. This was the place where he had wanted to be. He could wait and be patient, conquer loneliness, make good resolutions, and think of the future.

No doubt from time to time his speculating mind rested on a day three years ahead when he would come up for final examination. Proper examinations, which had fallen into disuse, had recently been revived again. Instead of a friendly glass of wine and a token question, there was now a grueling test, spoken and written, which lasted all day, from a bench of three examiners in the Schools, with all the rest of the university free to come in and watch from the public benches. To take a double first* in mathematics and classics was still rare, an honor to the student and an honor to his college.

Trinity at this time was very short of good students. It had the reputation of a "very gentlemanly college" and relied too heavily on gentleman commoners, young men of good family who paid double fees and therefore expected special treatment. The last thing they came to Oxford for was scholarship. They came to make the right friends, and to idle away,

*The distinction of obtaining a first-class honors degree in two different subjects.

very pleasantly to themselves and not too annoyingly to their families, the awkward years when they were past school and not ready for launching on the world. Under easy discipline, they could make their mistakes without falling too heavily on their aristocratic noses.

Trinity, however, was lately a little tired of its reputation as a suitable nursery for such young sprigs. It was trying to pull itself up by its own intellectual bootstraps, and a youngster like John Newman was a promise for the future. This was why, young though he was, they were glad to get him, although it is true they did not seem to do much about helping him once he was there.

At least, during those first tedious and trying three weeks, he could console himself with bright dreams. It was just as well that he could not look ahead three years, when the bright dreams of himself, his family, his college would all crash.

After three years of white hope, Newman of Trinity did not get a double first. In his final examination he broke down spectacularly, out of anxiety and overwork, and far from getting a double first, he did not even get second-class honors but came out, as they said, "under the line."

It was a desperate blow to his pride and to his career. By that time he was the only breadwinner and the family stood or fell by his efforts. Though it was not absolute failure, such a crash meant that he could hardly hope to rise in the Church or the law, the two learned professions, in one of which everyone had expected him to rise very high indeed.

"It is all over, and I have not succeeded."

4

The Oriel Examination

April 6, 1822

The day before Easter. Sun in the sky, daffodils in college gardens, beech trees flapping little green flags to welcome the spring, and all Oxford a dream of freshness and youth. To young men, clattering on horseback out of town that morning, or waiting at the King's Arms for the coach, there was a smell of cheerfulness in the air.

But not to John Henry Newman, the worst examination candidate in the world. From his shabby lodging-house bedroom, he could hear the noise of wheels and hoofs and loud voices from the inn yard, as though no one had a care in the world except himself.

Today was the beginning of the great five-day examination for the Oriel Fellowship, the most coveted prize in Oxford for an ambitious young man, in terms of money and a career. There was plenty of competition. Ten hopeful giants, already plumed with college honors, were to sit for it, and he, poor crazy under-the-liner, with nothing to his credit but a breakdown in the Schools, had decided to make the eleventh.

That disastrous final examination was eighteen months
behind him, but he was still living in Oxford, a member of
Trinity College. He was indeed rooted in, like the snapdragon on the walls. Where else in the world could John
Henry Newman think of living? As an undergraduate he had
been awarded a grant of £60 a year for nine years, so he cost
his family nothing, though it was not luxurious living. By
tutoring, he was even earning enough to have taken over
Frank's education as well. Frank lived with him now, studying for entrance to Worcester College, and promising well.

At least, on this anxious occasion, Frank had gone down
for the vacation, and that was something to be thankful for.
The brothers had their ups and downs together, and if the elder
had to sit with trembling fingers crooked round a coffee cup
from which he could hardly swallow a mouthful, he would
rather not be watched by his bouncy younger brother, who
might be bracing, or bored, but would certainly not be helpful.

John pushed his uneaten breakfast away and breathed
nervously on his glasses to polish them. The more he considered his chances, the sicker he felt.

John Henry Newman, twenty-one. That important date
had come and gone six weeks past, troubling him with the
thought that has assailed so many brilliant young men: that
he had reached this advanced age without making his mark
on the world. He noted in his diary: "My birthday. Today I
am of age. It is an awful crisis."

A long, cheerful, loving letter from his mother had not
helped at all. He had answered at his darkest and most de-
spairing: "Not that I am sorry so great a part of life is gone—
would that all were over!" Even allowing for his flowery style
and his tendency to exaggerated glooms, his mother was dis-

turbed. She wrote back hurriedly: "Take proper air and exercise; accept all the invitations you receive; and do not be overanxious about anything."

Advice more easily given than followed, that spring, taking into account John's temperament and the looming Oriel exam. He had been studying harder than ever these last months, and praying harder; neither made him feel any better; his mind turned in on itself like a whirlpool.

He prayed for success in the fellowship examination, of course. And then he prayed, not for success, but to do God's will. And then he prayed for success again. And then he renounced the idea of success. And then a cunning little watcher at the back of his mind suggested that God must be pleased with him for being so noble and would certainly give him the fellowship because he was so virtuously not asking for it. And so on, and so on. Yet, except for that outburst in his letter to his mother, he had not let on to anyone, particularly not to the brilliant and self-confident Frank, how his mind was giddying on its seesaw. He had seemed well, and cheerful, even casual, about the whole thing. He carried his temperamental difficulties out of sight, with courage, as some people carry bodily pain.

This morning it all caught up with him, as the Oxford clocks, in their staggering, haphazard fashion, chimed nine o'clock from all the points of the compass, spinning the whole affair out so long that it was almost time for the first one to start the quarter before the last one had finished with the hour.

John heard them as painfully as though they signaled his execution. He looked at the little pasteboard card on the table in front of him, bidding him attend at Oriel Hall by invitation of the Dean of Oriel at ten o'clock for the examination, and wondered whether the dreary pattern of the Schools was to be repeated, and whether he could survive another such disaster.

He gathered his resolution at the half hour and put on his cap and gown; picked up the card, the volume of the *Spectator* from which he would have to translate elegant English into elegant Latin, and his other belongings: pens, carefully cut the night before, penknife, pencil, and ruler; and marched down the stairs as bravely as he could manage.

The way to Oriel led past his own college, Trinity, and as he went by, a little picture flashed into his mind, uncalled. John Bowden, going through a craze for astronomy, had once dragged him up to Trinity tower to look at the stars through a new telescope. Bowden had muttered and grunted with enthusiasm, swiveling around the heavens with his eye to the eyepiece, wanting sympathy and getting none. John Newman was looking downward, leaning over the edge of the parapet, absorbed in the black shapes and yellow lights of the university buildings. He was thinking: "Which of these colleges will be mine in the end? Shall I live and die an Oxford don? Behind which walls? Under which tower?" Bowden, coming down from the planets, had rated him for a materialist. It was true that all the excitements of exploration were for him contained in a library, between the covers of a book.

At that time, even then, his ambitions had reached toward Oriel, although it was not very large and not much to look at. Visitors, trooping between the beauty of St. Mary's Church and the splendors of Christ Church and Merton Library, usually missed it altogether. They still do. But young men like John Newman would have given their ears for a fellowship there—would have given one ear for a single evening in the common room, just to hear the conversation of the fellows, reputed to be the best and most exciting conversation from the best minds in Oxford.

"Place stinks of logic," some people sniffed.

"Those fellows drink tea," sneered others, who still had a sort of last-century feeling that a gentleman ought to get soberly drunk every day after dinner, on a bottle of good port. Flippant undergraduates, hearty fellows with mud on their boots and guineas to spend on proper pleasures like horses and women, shouted: "Got the kettle boiling, porter?" as they passed the Oriel gate, and doubled up with laughter at the brilliance of their own joke.

But even they would have had to admit that if a man was inclined to scholarship, then a fellowship at Oriel meant the crown of a scholar's career and opened gates of endless possibility: Archbishop of Canterbury, Lord Chief Justice— who knew where it would end?

No wonder John went toward the examination hall twangling like a taut wire. In the narrow streets there were few people about, and no one wished him luck. But a shopkeeper or two, lounging at a doorway to look at the morning, eyed him. It was not their place to speak, but they knew him: of course they did. It was their job, since they lived by the university, to know every pale student who in a week's time might be a prosperous fellow of Oriel, a customer with money to spend.

He reached the college gate all too quickly. Over the arch there was a jutting window that marked the Tower Room. There, when the written papers were finished, next Wednesday, the candidates would be summoned for their orals in front of the assembled Fellows, to see which of them best came up to the college's demand for "Good Latin, good Greek, good English, and good sense."

Meanwhile, this Saturday morning, there were the English-into-Latin paper and the English essay, probably the two most important papers. The candidates came singly into the great hall, among them the university favorite, a man called Williams. Gossip said that he had been preparing for this moment by working fourteen hours a day for twelve months, living on beans and salad.

The Dean, great man, appeared on the dais to announce the rules of the examination and to hand out the questions. There was no time limit to the day's work, but candles were not allowed, so by half past six, when it would be getting dark, they would be forced to finish. Even so, it meant more than eight hours on hard benches, with minds at full stretch, as much a test of endurance as of intellect.

In silence the papers were handed around, and in silence the candidates worked, the long long silence of an examination room, broken by faint echoes of another world beyond the heavy oak door, and the scratching of quill pens.

John at least hardly noticed the passage of time. But when it was done, when in the last rays of light through the leaded window he had peered at his essay, crossing out a last word here, adding a comma there, he collapsed into depression. As he crawled off the hard bench, stiff all over, he knew beyond a doubt that he had made an irretrievable mess of both papers and that for a second time he was going to be defeated by his own overstrung mind.

He crept home and spent a miserable Easter Day. His stiffness got worse instead of better; he could not eat, could not sleep. Monday was a hell of blinding headache and despair, the smell of five hundred years of college dinners in the airless hall, and the remote faces of portraits on the wall sneering at him. He spent most of the afternoon with his eyes shut, not even thinking, and then woke to the fact that the darkness was closing in before he had corrected his Latin essay. He peered at it in panic, but the letters swam together in the dusk. The other candidates were filing out, and he had to hand in his essay uncorrected.

Another horrible night, and on Tuesday he really felt that his mind was going. It was dry and tight and tense—suppose he went mad suddenly, there in the hall? Suppose he died? It seemed quite possible. As soon as he bent his head to concentrate, his eyes seemed to turn around and inside out. He left the paper and walked up and down, up and down the hall, trying to piece together his sanity out of the splinters of an overworked brain.

On Wednesday afternoon was the oral, and Wednesday at midday John had a message to go to Trinity and see his tutor. He found Mr. Short eating an early dinner in his rooms, already in riding boots, just about to start for the country and his Easter vacation. The tutor looked sharply at his ghost of a pupil, all beaky nose and black-shadowed eyes, who folded up in a chair like a broken puppet and announced that he couldn't go on, that he would have to withdraw from the examination.

"We'll discuss that later," said Mr. Short briskly. "First, you'll have something to eat."

John did not want to eat, could hardly remember when he had wanted to eat last, but the tutor insisted, and once the plate was in front of him, the smell of lamb cutlets and fried parsley was better than he would have thought, was in fact

very good indeed. Suddenly he found himself ravenous, and
while he ate, answering questions between mouthfuls, Mr.
Short's soothing, sensible voice went on.

"And what did you put there? Yes . . . ye–es . . . very
good. Yes, I like that. And this tricky bit in line twenty? How
did you construe that? Oh, yes? Excellent! Excellent!"

The lamb cutlets disappeared down to insignificant bones.
John's spirits began to lift. Hope warmed him again, although
he did not know, and could not yet be told, that a deputation
of Oriel Fellows had been to Trinity that morning, inquiring
about this young Mr. Newman whose papers, so far, had
shown him to be way ahead of any other candidate.

He went back to Oriel for the rest of the exam, with a
very different view of things. The pendulum swung. John
Henry Newman the Dismal Failure vanished, and John
Henry Newman the Brilliant Scholar came uppermost. Looking around Oriel Hall, his eye caught and rested on, for the
first time, as if it had been suddenly put there for his comfort
by a kind God, a motto in the stained glass of one of the windows.

"Pie Repone Te"—"O righteous man, take heart.". . .

At moments of doubt and tension, John played his violin.
He played it in his sitting room that Friday morning, the bow
running so sweetly over the strings that he almost forgot, for
minutes together, what it was he was trying not to think about.

Then—a man at the door, let in by the landlady, who
smirked behind him. John's heart trying to take flight inside
his rib cage, until he thought it would succeed in bursting out.

"Deeply regret, sir, disagreeable news . . ."

A long pause, while the world turned slowly over and

came to rest again right side up. Well, it was only what he had known all along, and there was a relief in being certain of the worst.

". . . Mr. Newman is elected Fellow of Oriel, and his presence is required there immediately."

Then he remembered that it was traditional to deliver such messages in a topsy-turvy fashion, but he was furious with the impertinence of the man, standing there with a half smile, expecting to see him startled. Cold as ice, he tucked the violin under his chin again and played the last two bars over.

"Very well," he said coldly to the hovering servant, now looking nonplused.

"Mr. Newman? It is Mr. Newman?"

"It is, thank you." John won. He frowned in a considering manner at the score, and the man, beaten, with a backward glance, had to leave, unwelcomed and, worse, untipped.

John heard him down the stairs and out the door before he allowed himself to react. Then the violin was flung down, the music stand was knocked over, and he was off at a run, dragging on cap and gown between the top stair and the bottom.

The news, of course, was ahead of him, but as always he could not go out to meet other people's interest. He curled in on himself and strode down to Oriel with his chin dropped, looking neither right nor left, though shopkeepers, sure of him now, bowed from their doorways. Behind him, Trinity bells began to ring, the joyful clang and clash of a college that after many years had done something worthwhile in the university: it had fathered a Fellow of Oriel.

In the Tower Room over Oriel arch, there were none but

pleasant faces smiling a welcome to their newest, youngest recruit, who was too stiff with embarrassment to smile back.

"Congratulations, Newman," everyone said, stretching to take John's hand. Newman. Not *Mr.* Newman. At that proud moment it struck John with a painful thrill, as he took the hands and mumbled thanks, that he in turn would have to drop the "mister" and call these enormous, august scholars by their last names alone.

It was bearable, even the provost's dignity was bearable, until it came to the turn of John Keble, *the* John Keble, to John and to many others the greatest man in Oxford. Little and quiet, low-voiced and sweet-smiling, nonetheless he was a legend. Although he had never been to school, having received his education at home in his father's study, he had won a scholarship to Corpus Christi at the age of fourteen and taken a double first (the second in Oxford history) when he was seventeen. In the twelve months between his eighteenth and nineteenth birthdays, he had swept the Oxford board clean of prizes: a double first in classics and mathematics, both university essay prizes, the English and the Latin, and an open fellowship to Oriel. It was characteristic of John that far from being proud and excited to shake the hand of this intellectual star, he wished that the floor would open and let him fall through.

For the rest of the day, joy and agony tangled him in meshes. It was joy to confide to his diary: "I have this morning been elected a Fellow of Oriel. Thank God. Thank God." There was joy in taking his place in chapel and going through the ceremony after Evensong. The Junior Fellow took him by the hand and led him to the provost.

"Sir, what do you want?" is the Latin question.

"I seek the bounty of this college for a year," is the answer.

Then the newly made Fellow, on probation for a year, is led back to his seat, secure in the knowledge that unless he blots his copybook very badly, it is his safe seat forever.

There was joy in all this. But dinner, in silk stockings and knee breeches, was agony from end to end.

Everyone was most kind, in their fashion. But the common room was a booming babble of conversations in which he could not join. His head spun with wine, and ceremony, and so much silver plate, and so many dishes. He could not possibly be hungry, though he had to eat something, not even knowing what it was.

Worst of all, he was only the son of a failed banker. In his heart he was not sure of himself among gentlemen, over such giveaway trifles as table manners. There was a terrible occasion at dinner (not, we hope, on this first evening), when all was brought to a standstill as the distant, superimpressive provost uttered his name in rolling tones that stopped all conversation, seemed to stop the world, while the gentlemen commoners snickered. "Mr. Newman, we do *not* serve sweetbreads with a spoon. Manciple, bring a blunt knife."

But John Henry Newman, once a failure in the Schools, was on April 12, 1822, made a Fellow of Oriel College, Oxford. Nothing could blot that date out of the calendar. It was there, marked with a red flag, forever. When he was nearly eighty, he confessed, a little shyly, that he kept a small piece of wood from one of Oriel's worm-eaten beams, always on his bedside table.

5

The Clerk of Oxenford

One of the pleasanter characters in Chaucer's string of Canterbury pilgrims is the Clerk, a solemn young man with a single-minded thirst for learning.

> An *Oxford Cleric*, still a student though,
> One who had taken logic long ago,
> Was there; his horse was thinner than a rake,
> And he was not too fat, I undertake,
> But had a hollow look, a sober stare;
> The thread upon his overcoat was bare.
> He had found no preferment in the church
> And he was too unworldly to make search
> For secular employment. By his bed
> He preferred having twenty books in red
> Or black, of Aristotle's philosophy,
> To have fine clothes, fiddle, or psaltery.
> Though a philosopher, as I have told,
> He had not found the stone for making gold.
> Whatever money from his friends he took
> He spent on learning or another book
> And prayed for them most earnestly, returning
> Thanks to them thus for paying for his learning.
> His only care was study, and indeed
> He never spoke a word more than was need,

Formal at that, respectful in the extreme,
Short, to the point, and lofty in his theme.
The thought of moral virtue filled his speech,
And he would gladly learn, and gladly teach.*

Oxford, even at its lowest ebb, has always fathered a few of them. Allow for a difference of a few hundred years, and you have a very fair portrait of John Henry Newman, even to the story that Chaucer's clerk tells when his turn comes, which shows a high-minded ignorance of women.

Chaucer's clerk may even himself have been a member of Oriel College. The story does not say. If so, "to live and die a fellow of Oriel" was no doubt the sum of his ambitions, as it was of John Henry Newman's—to live just there, rooted like the snapdragon on the wall. For nine years after John's election, nothing much changed with him. There is no particular day to choose as typical. The best is to take a number of snapshots and come up, perhaps, with a composite picture.

See him then walking, a very young Bachelor of Arts, under the elms of Christ Church meadows, where donnish Oxford takes its mild exercise down by the river. On this occasion he is not alone but accompanied by a large rough man in a whitish overcoat, Richard Whateley, also of that college, better known as "The Great Bear"—a comment on his clothes, his enormous appetite, and his manners generally.

Whateley, however, odd though he might be, knew what it was to have suffered, in his time, agonies of shyness. Nowadays he didn't care, as he strode through the meadows, interrupting his flow of one-sided conversation to fling sticks for his dogs, which were as exuberant and rough-coated as him-

* From Nevile Coghill's translation of Chaucer's *Canterbury Tales*, quoted with the permission of the publishers, Penguin Books, Ltd.

self. People might think what they liked. His loud voice rolled on. He was, John wrote in his memoirs with a prim twinkle, "a great talker, who very readily endured the silence of his company."

There was method in these walks, however. Young Newman had already caused some anxious moments in the Oriel common room. The Fellows were somewhat dismayed—their new Fellow was so gawky and silent, and what was more, he actually played the fiddle in an amateur orchestra, not the occupation of a scholar and a gentleman. They wondered what they had got. Perhaps in choosing their candidate they had made a mistake, and would have done better to choose a safe double-first, as other colleges did. They told Whateley to take him in hand and see what there was behind that long nose and disconcerting stare.

It might not have worked for everybody, but under Whateley's rough but intensely logical tongue the new Fellow actually came out of his shell and was soon taking part in endless arguments. "Clearest-headed man I've met: don't you worry," was Whateley's comment. John was no fool—he knew just how much he owed to this eccentric, and though their ways parted, he felt a warm affection ever after for the man who "first gave me heart to look about me, after my election, and taught me to think correctly, and . . . to rely upon myself."

Turn over a page and see him on his ordination day. The demand of God on him, which he never ceased to feel as an urgent, absolute, personal call, could only be fulfilled by going into the Church.

"Make me thy instrument . . . make use of me, when thou wilt, and dash me to pieces when thou wilt. Let me, living or dying, in fortune and misfortune, in health and sickness, in honour and dishonour, be thine," he wrote in his diary. It was a marriage vow, and more than marriage.

Even so, the day itself caught him almost unawares. When the moment came to kneel and hear the solemn words, he began to breathe short and fast, almost ready to faint. Some in that group of clever young men might take this moment very easily, no doubt did—after all, ordination was the easy key to so many ladders of advancement—but not John Henry Newman, whose God had long ago laid a finger on him and now spoke through the solemn, magnificent words of the Prayer Book.

"Again we exhort you, in the name of Our Lord Jesus Christ, that you have in remembrance"—the Bishop's voice might be merely human, he might cough, or look aside, or slur his words, or think of his dinner or his wife, but John Henry Newman heard the voice of God—"that you have in remembrance, into how high a dignity and to how weighty an office and charge ye are called; that is to say, to be messengers, watchmen, and stewards of the Lord; to teach, and to premonish, to feed and provide for the Lord's family; to seek for Christ's sheep that are dispersed abroad, and for his children who are in the midst of this naughty world, that they may be saved through Christ for ever."

Forever. In at least one heart those words tolled like a great bell. John was suddenly overtaken with fear, and shuddered, like a man plunged into deep cold water.

" 'For ever'—words never to be recalled. I have the responsibility of souls on me to the day of my death."

He preached his first sermon on the text: "Man goeth forth to his work and to his labour until the evening." It was not a very good sermon, but the text was typical. John himself was a compulsive worker, and any picture album must show one shot of him bent over his books in the "brown room" looking over Oriel quadrangle. Now the whole family depended on him—Frank while he was still a student; his mother and three sisters after his father's death; poor demented Charlie, who could never keep a job but was adept at scrounging money out of his brothers; dear Aunt Betsy, whose affairs were always in a tangle. He had to add to his fellowship by private coaching, by writing.

It was not only, or perhaps not mainly, the need for money which drove him to four hours' sleep a night and something near a stomach ulcer. He almost managed to ruin his health before he was thirty—how and why, one asks, against that quiet, sober background, that peaceful college retreat?

Read his own description of how he wrote: "I write, I write again: I write a third time in the course of six months." (No typewriters, of course, and every quill to be cut by hand and constantly sharpened.) "Then I take the third: I literally fill the paper with corrections, so that another person could not read it. I then write it out fair for the printer. I put it by; I take it up; I begin to correct again; it will not do. Alterations multiply; pages are rewritten, little lines sneak in and crawl about. The whole page is disfigured; I write again; I cannot count how many times this process is repeated."

He once worked all day in college, then settled down, until four in the morning, to an article he was writing for the *Encyclopedia Metropolitana,* and as it was then hardly worthwhile going to bed, he blew out the candle, took his overcoat and stick, and walked eighteen miles to have breakfast with a friend.

There was an absolute determination within him that he must do his best, that if he were not at full stretch, using every last volt of energy, he was not doing enough. It was better to be exhausted than to feel guilty. And yet this was not ordinary ambition. The kingdom of scholarship was his only kingdom. "I think I really desire the truth," he said.

"One thing I have earnestly desired for years, and I trust with sincerity—that I may never be rich; and I will add (though here I am more sincere at some times than at others) that I may never rise in the church."

There spoke Chaucer's clerk, only from the nineteenth century instead of the fourteenth. But Chaucer's clerk, I suspect, after his one brief outing to Canterbury retired into his college rooms and was never heard of again until he blinded his eyes poring over black-letter folios. Newman will be heard of, but not yet. He is not yet a leader, only a scholar, tutor, friend, brother, son.

No picture is complete without seeing him as brother and son—so responsible, and still, at this stage, entirely satisfactory. "Dear John Henry . . . my guardian angel," his mother spoke of him. Sometimes, as mothers will, she imagined him happily married (though, like many others, she would almost certainly not have approved of his choice). He did not think this likely, though as yet he had no settled views on celibacy. But the physical side of sex meant very little to him; as a Fellow of his college he could not marry yet, and if he remained a scholar at Oxford he could never marry; his love for his sisters took his tenderness, particularly his love for the adored youngest, the bright and charming and altogether delightful Mary. Sometimes he wondered if he channeled too much love toward them, whether this would not be punished:

his God was a jealous God as well as a loving one, who would intervene to snatch away the toy that the child sets his heart on overmuch. The picture is not a pleasant one, but there were deep shadows in John Henry's religion, and at its best, without the shadows, it was still tough. He wrote in his diary:

"Those who make comfort the great subject of their preaching seem to mistake the end of their ministry. *Holiness* is the great end. There must be a struggle and toil here. Comfort is a cordial, but no one drinks cordials from morning to night."

There would never be much comfort for him, he was not built that way. He would inch doggedly along his own road, his only road, out into a bleak landscape, to find the truth as he saw the truth, no matter where it might lead him.

One can readily imagine that there would be clashes on the way, and the clashes soon came. It is comic, and a little sad, to see him wrestling in his diary with such knotty problems as: "I *must* find some way to explain to the Fellows about my wish to keep Sunday holy"—how to get out of going to the Provost's Sunday breakfast parties without sounding too much of a prig, he meant.

"Pound me, Lord, into small bits, grind me down, anything for a meek and quiet spirit." The Lord seems to have been only too ready to oblige.

However, Oriel, once it got used to young Mr. Newman, thought highly of him and appointed him a tutor. He was now in charge of undergraduates, as Mr. Short of Trinity had been in charge of him. Being John Henry Newman, he saw his responsibilities as more than supplying sympathy and lamb cutlets. He felt the deepest interest in the salvation of their souls: tutoring, to him, was a priestly task—his group of students were his parish.

Fireworks were inevitable, for Oriel, like Trinity, had its quota of gentlemen commoners, gay young blades most comically remote from everything that their new tutor stood for.

Read that entertaining old novel, *Tom Brown at Oxford,* for a description of one of their famous breakfasts. (Dinner had to be eaten in Hall; so breakfast, at ten or eleven in the morning, was the undergraduate's best chance of entertaining his friends.)

> Every morning the boy from the Weirs arrived with freshly caught gudgeon, and now and then an eel or trout, which the scouts on the staircase had learnt to fry delicately in oil. Fresh watercresses came in the same basket, and the college kitchen furnished a spitchcocked chicken or grilled turkey's legs. In the season there were plovers' eggs; or, at the worst, there was a dainty omelette; and a distant baker, famed for his light rolls and high charges, sent in the bread—the common domestic college loaf being of course out of the question with any one with the slightest pretensions to taste, and fit only for the perquisite of scouts. Then there would be a deep Yorkshire pie, or reservoir of potted game, as pièce de résistance, and a large cool tankard of cider or ale-cup to finish up with, or soda-water and maraschino for a change. Tea and coffee were there indeed, but they were rarely touched. . . . Ready money was plenty and credit good, and they might have had potted hippopotamus for breakfast if they had chosen to order it, which they most likely would have done if they had thought of it.

One can imagine how John, perhaps no farther off than in the rooms above such a splendid party, drinking his tea and eating his slice of "the common domestic college loaf," with his nose in a book, was appalled. It was all frivolity and no work, and irresponsibility—not, in his view, what colleges had been built for at all. And there were worse things than this. One of them was the way in which the communion service was celebrated in the college chapel once each term.

It has to be remembered that membership in the established Church was obligatory for every member of the university. Students could be sent down, older members dismissed, for unorthodoxy. Frank Newman was one who suffered: after a brilliant double first, he had to refuse his degree because he could not honestly swear to the Thirty-nine Articles of the Church of England. By that time, other universities were being founded, and he ended up as a professor at London University, which had no religious qualifications.

In Oxford colleges the termly communion was obligatory and by tradition had become an occasion to be celebrated. The bright young men went to communion in a spirit that had very little to do with religion, and went straight on to champagne breakfasts, at which they got roaring drunk. Newman, horrified, applied to the head of the college to find out whether it was absolutely necessary for these irreligious young men to go to the sacrament, and found himself banging his head against the stone wall of tradition. "That question, I believe," said the provost, "has never entered their heads, and I beg you will not put it into them."

You have to see both sides. The introduction of a note of religious fervor where it has not existed before is a highly uncomfortable, even dangerous process. Anyway, all young men are hotheaded. In time, Newman's ideas would cool down from fervor to decency. So thought the provost.

Meanwhile, some of the undergraduates flourished under his tuition. It was a selective form of education. Those who were good students, who wanted to learn, who were willing to be influenced, had every care lavished on them. Those who did not cooperate could scramble through as they might.

In the end he lost his tutorship because the provost could not approve his methods, but the "Oriel group" had begun to be heard of outside the college walls. They were a cluster of bright stars.

There was John Keble, eldest of them, brilliant, gentle, quiet, quite obviously a saint to anyone who knew him. He was not seen in Oxford so much now, having married and retired to a country parsonage (headship of a college was almost the only "marriageable" post within the university). He found national fame almost overnight as the author of *The Christian Year,* a book of poems that ran into ninety-two editions in its author's lifetime.

There was Hurrell Froude, the explosive, lovable, lively Froude. ("You know the story of the murderer who has done one good deed in his life? My one good deed was to bring Keble and Newman together.") Tall, thin, gay, and noisy, always shocking solemn older dons with outrageous opinions and high-colored slang, quite capable of climbing Oriel gate like an undergraduate if he had stayed out after locking-up time; so excited when he got his fellowship that he rushed out on the town and got drunk; a hard rider, who took fences as he took ideas, at full tilt. He knew his place in the group as the ginger man: "Keble is my fire, but I am his poker." Underneath it all there lay a deep seriousness, and somewhere in his physical make-up the germs of tuberculosis, which killed him when he was thirty-three.

There were others: Robert Wilberforce, Marriott, the Mozley brothers, Isaac Williams. And there was John Newman. Those who did not like him hardly noticed him, because if he had nothing to say he kept silence. To some of the wild young men of Oriel, he was only a quiet tutor on whom they played tricks, although even then they were sometimes surprised.

"What did he say to you?" one undergraduate asked another, a rather shaken young man emerging from Newman's room after being reprimanded.

"I don't know, but he looked at me."

"A tutor with whom men did not venture to take liberties," another of them remembered, "and who was master of a formidable and speaking silence calculated to quell any ordinary impertinence."

Some felt this quality only as a negative, a "formidable and speaking silence." To others it was an electric spark which they did not forget, could not, because by it they caught fire.

"It never was possible to be even a quarter of an hour in his company without a man feeling himself incited to take an onward step, sufficient to tax his energies or his faith."

People begin now to look up in the streets, and nudge one another, as he passes, with his head down and his eyes fixed a thousand miles ahead, and they say, "That's Newman of Oriel," as he and Bowden had once said, "That's Keble." A man perhaps born to be the leader of a movement, if circumstances provide him with a movement which he cares to lead.

6

Far from Home

March 3, 1833

A post chaise rattling on the road from Naples to Rome, along the ancient paving of the Via Appia. Through old towns, their streets of modern houses interrupted by Roman ruins; over the Pontine Marshes; through a hilly district of wild woods and rocks where the postilions looked over their shoulders for robbers; down from the hills and across the deserted flats called the Campagna, with the walls and domes of the city of Rome beginning to show in the distance.

The Campagna struck many travelers even more than the city itself—miles of desolation, where cloaked shepherds herded sheep among the ruins of an ancient civilization: broken pillars, empty tombs, the arches of old aqueducts staggering across the landscape; an isolation of ruins in the gathering darkness. You looked no farther, it was the complete symbol of a fallen civilization.

The English travelers, as they had been warned, pulled up the windows of their chaise to keep out the dangerous fever-laden night air; the *bad air*, it was called, the *malaria,*

which rose from swamp and stagnant water. Keep the air out
and you kept out the fever, a prescription that worked very
well because so far nobody had linked fever with the bites of
the mosquitoes that were also kept out by closed windows.

"It is a fitting approach to a city which has been the scene
of divine judgements."

One line out of a letter is enough to date our travelers,
and almost to add the signature, John Henry Newman. It was
typical of both the time and the man to feel that jealous God
breathing close behind his shoulder, ready to revenge himself
for their own good on those who stepped out of line. Rome, of
course, had stepped very far out of the line of pure faith en-
trusted to her nineteen centuries before. But if Rome had
erred, where was the truth to be found? This was the problem to which John and his fellow thinkers, Keble, Hurrell
Froude, and the rest of them, were devoting themselves with
passionate single-mindedness. For them, religious truth could
be discovered, and must be discovered, at the cost of any
sacrifice. Like explorers looking for the source of the Nile,
they ventured further and further into dangerous realms of
thought, forging along almost untrodden ways, determined,
and terrified, for they did not know where their journey would
end; they only knew they had to go.

Newman, now thirty-two, was going back to the grass
roots, already deep in studies of the fathers of the early
Church. His first sight of the city of Rome—knowing what
we know about his future—has to be important. If he had
said nothing at all in his letters and diaries, we should be
spinning theories. But in fact he said a lot. Nothing else in
his life struck him like his first view of the great city, the
eternal city, the first of cities (no names were too grand).

Three cultures—the Roman, the Renaissance, the Christian, one on top of the other, lavishly encrusted—gave a wealth of richness to the experience.

In all his long life, Newman made one journey—this trip in 1833, with Hurrell Froude and Hurrell's father—to the Mediterranean. Everything else that ever happened to him happened either in the world of ideas or else in human relationships. Just this once he had a physical adventure, and the effect on this very sensitive and introverted person was staggering.

In *Wuthering Heights,* Cathy says: "I've dreamed in my life dreams that have stayed with me ever after, and have changed my ideas: they've gone through and through me, like wine through water, altered the colour of my mind." And that is the only way to describe John Newman's quiet trip, three sightseeing clergymen going the round of the Mediterranean.

There was only one way to cope with so much new experience. He wrote and wrote and wrote. Letters poured out of him like water from a broken pipe. Writing everything down, analyzing and describing, catching the flash and glitter of changing emotions, was the only way he could organize his chaotic sensations. As he looked at Homer's Greek islands, at St. Paul's Malta, at the early Christians' Rome, his sensitive imagination could hardly bear the impact of it all. It became positively painful; he longed to be away, to *have* seen it all, to be back in the quiet brown room at Oriel, with his feet up on the sofa, where he could think through and organize and enjoy his memories. Their actuality was too bright. He suffered, as you might imagine the sensitized film suffers while the photograph is actually being taken and the whole world flashes in instantaneously through the shutter.

"I only endure the sights, and had much rather *have* seen them than see them, though the while I am extremely astonished and almost enchanted at them." "I long to be back, yet wish to make the most of being out of England, for I never wish to leave it again." "I never loved home so well as now I am away from it—and the exquisite sights which foreign countries supply both to the imagination and the moral taste are most pleasurable in *memory,* but scarcely satisfactory as a present enjoyment."

What do we make of such a traveler? He seems to be one skin short, like an albino, in need of dark glasses to shield the glare. "I did not know before, the mind could be so excited in so many various ways; but it is as much so as if one were literally pulled about, and had now a leg twitched and now one's head turned."

If that was true of lesser places, of Corfu and the Aegean Islands and Malta, what of Rome now?

It sent him into an extraordinary state of mind.

"What can I say of Rome, but that it is the first of cities, and that all I ever saw are but as dust (even dear Oxford inclusive) compared with its majesty and glory." "Of course I have seen very little of it; but the effect of every part is so vast and overpowering—there is such an air of greatness and repose cast over the whole, and, independent of what one knows from history, there are such traces of long sorrow and humiliation, suffering, punishment and decay, that one has a mixture of feelings, partly such as those with which one would approach a corpse, and partly those which would be excited by the sight of the spirit which had left it."

He fell in love with Rome, and yet it had to represent something he hated, the Roman Church. Other people might have solved this clash somehow at a fairly shallow level, but Newman was both too sensitive and too honest. The letters poured out to his mother, his sisters, his friends, and no doubt Hurrell and he sat up talking till the small hours.

He walked in St. Peter's, feeling himself "little and contemptible" because of the size and beauty of the place. "When you get aloft and look down inside the Dome, then you see what a mountain the building is." And yet this magnificent mountain was built on error and financed by the sale of indulgences to the poor and credulous all over Europe. Ideas, emotions, education, prejudices, belief—the very foundation on which he rested was taking a beating, a heavier beating even than he realized at the time.

"It is impossible to enter into the full power of what one sees at once—the sights of celebrated places are like seeds sown in the mind."

The journey had come about because Hurrell, with a cough that would not clear, had been advised to try wintering in a more southerly climate. Newman, thin with overwork as usual, had been persuaded to go along. At first he refused. The thought alarmed him. Had it been written already, he might have quoted Browning's poem:

> And I'm the weak-eyed bat no sun should tempt
> Out of the grange whose four walls make his world.

But once the idea had been dropped into his mind, he was bound to go. Arguments cropped up. It would be good for his health. It was a chance to extend his education that might never come again. It might break his shyness, make him more at ease with learned and traveled men. To some extent, all this was rationalization. This journey, coming at mid-

career, would also let him stand back, take a long look at himself, find out which way he was facing and whether it was the
right way. If, as seemed more and more likely, he and Keble
and Froude and some others had a monster of a task ahead of
them, an appraisal was essential. Because it looked as though
the work they had to do was to get the whole Church of England into better shape, in the teeth of its dug-in establishment, clean out its errors and make it more like the house of
God it had to be.

It is a human characteristic to feel drawn into the desert
at the start of a great enterprise, there to thrash out one's problems alone, and stand one's temptations. Newman not only
withdrew from his familiar background for the Mediterranean
trip. Compulsively, and not understanding himself, he then
let the Froudes go home alone while he started on a trip into
Sicily.

"Among strangers into a wild country to live a wild life,
to travel in solitudes and to sleep in dens of the earth—and all
for what? For the gratification of an imagination, for the idea
of a warm fancy which might be a deceit, drawn by a strange
love of Sicily to gaze upon its cities and mountains."

He said goodbye to the Froudes, saw them off to the
South of France, and took the opposite road to Sicily, loaded
with "curry powder, spice, pepper, salt, sugar, tea and ham;
cold cream, a straw hat, and a map of Sicily. I shall want
nothing from the island but macaroni, honey and eggs."

What in fact he got from the island was a bad bout of
fever which nearly killed him.

It was the beginning of May, and although he tried for
many years to disentangle the next six weeks, the effort was
never completely successful. It was like a book that has got

wet, and the pages cannot afterwards be pulled apart without much tearing and spoiling.

May 2—that was the first day. He remembered that afterwards all right, very vividly. It was a strikingly beautiful but not a happy day. He went forty-two miles, mostly on muleback, sometimes getting off to walk beside the animal. He was stiff and miserable and headachy, which he thought was due to the long journey, but in fact the fever was on him already. If he had been a more experienced traveler, he would have been suspicious the night before: all the inns seethed with fleas and bugs, but he wasn't bitten. He accepted this as a welcome relief, not knowing that it was a sign of fever.

The scenery he rode through was very beautiful. The green corn of all shades was fever-bright in his eyes, rippling like watered silk over the hillsides, with the light-brown bones of the island sticking up raw between the green patches. There were deep valleys and high hills, and in the distance behind them, Etna's cone still visible, and little stone-walled towns perched on the tops of hills, protected from robbers, open to the light and the wind.

It was all so beautiful that, unexpectedly, the beauty moved him to tears. It somehow brought back his great sorrow, five years past but as bitter as ever. In one devastating twenty-four hours, with no warning, they had lost Mary, the baby, the darling, the gayest and most gifted of them all, who shone, as some few people do, across all their lives. Hurrell Froude was another who was often described as "shining," and he too was soon to die. In his life, John was to lose most of the people he really loved, peeled away one after the other like the protective skins of an onion, leaving him always more alone, more vulnerable, and shrinking further inside himself.

Mary had died between a night and a morning—of appendicitis, a heart disease? Nobody seems to have put a name to it. She felt ill as she ate turkey at dinner one Christmas holiday, went early to bed, passed a miserable night, died at noon. She was nineteen. The somber side of John's religion had often given him a presentiment that he loved her too much, that she was bound to be taken by the jealous God who disciplined his people so. He cried for her until he was over eighty. He cried now, looking at a landscape so fresh and innocent in its spring beauty that it looked like the garden of Eden.

Next morning, after a sleepless, feverish night full of troubled dreaming, the details of which he later forgot, he could not get out of bed but rolled over helplessly against the pillows.

Luckily for him, the Italian servant he had hired for the journey was stolidly goodhearted and had an old soldier's knowledge of how to treat a fever. He saved John's life, over the next three weeks.

Afterwards deeply moved by the feeling that he had been through some extraordinary experience and had emerged with life and future not only intact but brighter and more purposeful, John tried to pick apart the gummed-up leaves of memory. A number of pictures came to light, but the narrative was never quite complete. By that time, of course, he was back in England, and the only person who could have helped him untangle it all, Gennaro, was at home in Naples.

There was more than one inn, that was certain. In the early stages of the illness, Gennaro had urged him on, literally holding him on the mule sometimes, letting him lie in the shade at midday, feeding him bits of cooked chicken, oranges, or toast and water, trying to get on, before his pa-

tient collapsed completely, to some more civilized town with
a doctor.

There was a doctor, a doctor who could only talk Italian,
so they had to communicate as best as they could in Latin,
rusty student's Latin on the doctor's side, scholar's Latin humming with fever on John's.

There were all those long days and nights when in the
dreamy confusion of delirium he seemed to be sitting on endless staircases, aching for something that never happened;
there was pain and fever, and the drumming of his mind
telling him that it was all his own fault, that he had brought
this on himself by wicked obstinacy. There were times when
feebly he challenged Gennaro's remedies and wanted something different, which was kept from him, and he struggled
helplessly. There were deep deserts of loneliness and fear. "I
felt God was fighting against me . . . I seemed to see more and
more my utter hollowness. . . . I compared myself with Keble,
and felt that I was merely developing his, not my convic-
tions. . . ."

But through it all there was a fixed determination that he
would not die. Gennaro said quite openly that he was dying,
and being a practical man, thought that at least John might
make a will, leaving him the baggage in return for his loy-
alty, but John kept murmuring: "I have not sinned against
the light. I shall not die. I have not sinned against the light,"
as though death, with its end to work almost before work had
started, must be a punishment, and one which, bad though he
was, he had not quite merited.

There were days in the fever when every nerve ending
was unnaturally sensitive, his skin hardly able to bear the
touch of blankets; light was blinding, and every slight sound

reverberated in his hollow head; voices outside his door, or the ringing of the church bells, became physical agony. Many times worse, it was the same sense of impending madness that he had had in Oriel Hall during the exam for the fellowship. Frightened of himself, he took to counting the stars and flowers on the wallpaper—anything to push away the threatening breakdown.

Gennaro took everything in his stride. "If I get the fever, I get it," he said stolidly. But he didn't, and John at last, on some day or night that he could not remember at all, passed the crisis and began to recover. In the aftermath of fever the unnatural sensitivity was sometimes a blessing. Though noise was still torture, sometimes the cool smell of a camomile flower, or the taste of freshly brewed tea, gave him such exquisite pleasure that he cried out with delight. As soon as he was halfway strong enough, Gennaro got him going again on the road to Palermo.

"My joy was too great for me at first. I never saw such a country—the spring in its greatest luxuriance. All sorts of strange trees—very steep and high hills over which the road went; mountains in the distance—a profusion of aloes along the road. Such bright colouring—all in tune with my reviving life."

All that Gennaro asked for, as a souvenir of their eventful month together, was the old blue cloak. It would have been a poor present, no doubt John said to himself, rationalizing his refusal and giving Gennaro £10 over his wages instead, and a letter of gratitude which might serve him in the future. After such an adventure, he could not part with the one material memento of it: years later, he still spread that old cloak on his bed on cold nights.

Now he could not wait to get home. At Palermo he caught an orange boat bound for Marseilles, and it lay becalmed for a week in the Mediterranean, a trial he could hardly bear.

He sat on deck, still very weak from his illness, and watched the summer sea and sky as the dusk drew down, the shore lights winking in the distance. He ached with homesickness. But for which home? That journey into the shadows had brought God closer still. John had never, since childhood, quite believed in the reality of material things ("What a veil and curtain this world of sense is! Beautiful, but still a veil"). He had not changed much from the boy who rested in the thought of "two and two only supreme and luminously self-evident beings, myself and my Creator."

It was a habit with him to write verse for his recreation, when he was shaving, or slightly seasick, or bored with traveling long distances by coach. To pass the time on that quiet sea, he pulled out his pencil and notebook.

> Lead, kindly Light, amid the encircling gloom,
>   Lead thou me on!
> The night is dark, and I am far from home,
>   Lead thou me on!
> Keep thou my feet; I do not ask to see
> The distant scene—one step enough for me.
>
> I was not ever thus, nor prayed that thou
>   Shouldst lead me on.
> I loved to see and choose my path, but now
>   Lead thou me on!
> I loved the garish day, and spite of fears,
> Pride ruled my will; remember not past years.

So long thy power hath blest me, sure it still
    Will lead me on
O'er moor and fen, o'er crag and torrent, till
    The night is gone;
And with the morn those angel faces smile
Which I have loved long since, and lost awhile.

Three weeks later he arrived in England, and the very same Sunday Keble preached a sermon in St. Mary's, Oxford, "On National Apostasy," in which he reproached England with having lost its respect for the English Church. Although nobody much noticed it at the time, it has always been counted as the kicking-off point, the starting whistle, for the Oxford Movement.

7

The Oxford Movement

A Sunday evening in the spring of 1836

The bells of Oxford are summoning people to church. Trickles of people, both town and gown, tall hats and silk bonnets and flat scholars' caps, converging on that point in the broad curve of the High Street where stands the University Church, which is also the parish church of St. Mary's. Tonight, as almost every Sunday, the vicar is to preach, and the vicar is John Henry Newman.

St. Mary's is at the center of any map of Oxford, and it has always been at the center of university affairs. The first church, we are told, was built on the site in the time of Alfred the Great, so it has been long enough for things to happen there. It used to be the only place of meeting for the scholars, their only library and storehouse, but that was hundreds of years ago. They have built a different church since then, with barley-sugar pillars to its porch and an elaborate crocketed spire. But time moves slowly in Oxford. Nobody has yet mended the pillar that was cut about to allow room for the dock at the trial of Archbishop Cranmer and his companions in 1555. The statue of the Virgin and Child over the

doorway carries the marks of the Puritan bad temper of one
of Cromwell's troopers. Wesley seems to have stood up to
preach only last week, and Keble's sermon of 1833, which
counts as a convenient beginning to the Oxford Movement,
is hardly more than a matter of yesterday. The close-packed
congregation on this Sunday evening is not thinking that it
has any particular place in history, but it has. To have heard
John Henry Newman preach in St. Mary's, Oxford, allows
each of them the right to a footnote in history, at least.

These are still the great days of the Oxford Movement.
As Tom Mozley said when he was an old man: "Men survive, or have but lately passed away, who can never have
known what it was to share a glory and a greatness except at
that happy time."

Under the chancel arch and into the body of the church
steps the Vicar of St. Mary's, a tall, thin, gowned figure, a
little stooped, walking very quickly and as though folded into
his own thoughts, so that he arrives before you have time to
say, "He's here," and is up the steps of the high pulpit before
the congregation has rustled itself into a comfortable position
for listening.

They stir expectantly, particularly the ranks of undergraduates who have come too late for seats and stand tight-
packed under the shadow of the gallery, missing their dinner
in college in order to hear the man they believe in before all
others. ("Credo in Newmannum"—"I believe in Newman"—
is the slogan, and the Heads of Houses, mistrusting such
dangerous stuff, have changed college dinner hours so that
you can hear Newman or have dinner, but not both.)

The sermon begins. Don't expect fireworks and dramatic
gesture. This is a quiet, somber man ("a poor-looking, pinched-

up person," says a lady visitor, her hopes blighted), with the lights near him turned down low because his eyes hurt, reading a written sermon from a sheaf of manuscript, in a low voice. Some people, who come expecting to be carried away by a real hell-raiser, are sadly disappointed; they say his delivery is dull and meaningless. But once that voice catches you, as it has caught many of those young men at the back, you never forget it, for good or ill.

Instead of dramatics, and the special religious voice, they hear a man speak as though he were really thinking about what he says before he says it. That is rare enough. Although the words are written, he pauses as though to test the rightness of what he says. When he riffles through his Bible and produces a quotation to point the sentence, it is as though that verse, for just that purpose, has burst on him now, instantaneously, with a flash of inspiration. He means every word. The low clear voice may lack fire, but it reaches every corner of the church, the last row of pews, and it reaches into hearts and calls them.

"He effaced himself," said one of the earnest young men who heard him. "It was like God speaking to you."

People are lucky who, while they are young and impressionable, have the experience of meeting just one person with something of that power. . . . "That voice so keen, so preternaturally sweet, whose very whisper used to thrill through crowded churches, when every breath was held to hear; that calm grey eye; those features, so stern, and yet so gentle!"

Exaggerated, of course. A little more humor and a little less hero worship would perhaps have made a better mixture. But the point is not whether Newman was really like that, but why it was that to half a generation of young Oxford men he *seemed* like that. They paid him, of course, the usual compliment of imitating him, so that Oxford seemed to be full of men who held their heads slightly to one side, spoke in very soft voices, quickly and with long pauses between the sentences. You could tell the real followers by these mannerisms, especially in church, where, said an observer sardonically, they all "fell on their knees exactly as if their legs were knocked out from under them."

Nobody has ever quite explained, and it's too late now, the eyewitnesses being all long dead, the extraordinary power that Newman wielded. Reading about him is like hearing people talk of the marvelous actors who trod the stages of their youth. You have to take the descriptions on trust—there is no way of checking back. Least of all, is it any good to read through a dozen volumes of his sermons in print, hoping to be moved. A few readers can still find some faint magic here and there. The rest of us dip in, and not being theologians, wonder what all the fuss was about.

That it was about something real, we must believe. The quality was there, and at the time it was almost as powerful in print as in church. The sermons were best-sellers.

Most of all, perhaps, it was the true leader's quality of making people feel under a compulsion to reach for the highest that was in them.

"What have we ventured for Christ?" was the theme of one of these Sunday evening sermons.

"Our duty lies in risking upon Christ's word what we have, for what we have not; and doing so in a noble, generous way, not indeed rashly or lightly, still without knowing accurately what we are doing, not knowing either what we give up, nor again what we shall gain." (Thinking perhaps, as he said the words, of Hurrell, who after three years' gallant fight against his enemy, had just died. "When I took leave of him his face lighted up and almost shone in the darkness, as if to say that in this world we were parting for ever.") "Not knowing either what we give up, nor again what we shall gain; uncertain about our reward, uncertain about our extent of sacrifice, in all respects leaning, waiting upon Him, trusting in Him to fulfill His promise, trusting in Him to enable us to fulfill our own vows, and so in all respects proceeding without carefulness or anxiety about the future."

And young men left the church, with their lives changed, swept off their feet by a vision of golden opportunity. "He spoke with such piercing insight that you thought the secrets of your own heart had been revealed to him."

By this year, 1836, the pattern of Newman's life was made and fixed; the trip to Sicily had been the last ingredient poured in before the mold hardened. The pattern of his human relationships, too—that would not considerably change in the future except by further loss.

Both his sisters, Harriet and Jemima, married this year, married the two Mozley brothers, who had been John's students and remained his friends. Frank and Charles had wandered away from the family circle. Mary was dead and always missed. His mother died suddenly a few weeks after Hurrell, and now there was no longer a family home, and John lived entirely in Oriel, settled into a lonely bachelorhood.

Nobody would ever know how much he missed Hurrell, but his mother's death had shaken him more. He had not expected it, and of late they had drifted apart, and he blamed himself.

Such things, as usual, are no one's fault. When John was

first ordained, his mother and sisters were pleased and proud. They eagerly asked for his advice, embroidering the priest on to the son and brother. He sent them copies of his sermons and they read them aloud on Sunday afternoons; when the sisters were confirmed, they came up to Oxford especially to receive communion first from his hand.

But as he ploughed along the line of his studies, his picture of the Church changed radically and the three women found him going further and further away from them. It mattered to them all so much when their religious opinions could not coincide. More than it should, no doubt; more than we can imagine now; but it was the climate of the times. (When Frank turned agnostic, John would not meet his brother or dine with him.)

But lay aside the matter of religious opinions and there was still John's inhibited temperament to deal with. An odd little occurrence is revealing. At home one day, overworked and overtired as usual, he fainted, and there was a general rush to get him lifted on to the sofa. He came to, half-muzzy, to find his mother picking up his feet, a gesture he could not accept from her, and he jumped up and pulled away, leaving her hurt and mortified. He was miserable, but he could not explain—there was nothing to explain, he was made that way and that was all. It was a little thing, but important. After her death, the scene came back to him over and over again—it summed up all the ways in which he felt he had let her down, been less than the son he ought to have been.

"I am not more lonely than I have been for a long while," he wrote to Jemima after the funeral. "God intends me to be lonely."

And it was a very remote and lonely figure, the captain

of the ship, the hero on a pedestal ("King of Oxford," he had been nicknamed), who stood up in the gray gloom of St. Mary's pulpit, reading low and rapidly from his manuscript sermon.

That was the leader, but what was the Movement he led?

It was called the Oxford Movement quite simply because it originated in Oxford, the Tractarian Movement because much of what it had to say was distributed by tracts, the New-manites or the Puseyites because these were the names most often associated with the leadership.

It is not easy to explain in a few words what these men were trying to do, what they felt they were called to do. Per-haps the best way is to go back to the novels of Jane Austen, who died before the Movement began. Half the young men in her books are clergymen—the army, the navy, the law, and the church being the only genteel professions—and there is no difference that we can see, in those quiet, leisured circles, between the clergymen and the others. Their days pass in riding, reading, visiting, picnicking, dancing, sketching, and, of course, getting married. It is all cool, low-pitched, and per-fectly proper. *Religion,* it seems, in any sense in which we understand the word, would be totally out of place.

Enthusiasm has never been a word of praise among the English upper classes, who have made a virtue of hiding their emotions and carrying everything lightly. A church, therefore, in which all the clergy came from this class was not exactly fervent. You spoke to God as one gentleman to another. He understood your point of view and you did not embarrass each other by any vulgarity. (It is worth adding that not only the Church of England was like this. We should hardly recog-

nize the old English version of Roman Catholicism without its
Italian and Irish influences: priests wore plain clothes and
were addressed as "Mr."; chapels were severely plain and un-
adorned; statues, rosaries, hymn singing, and all the other
trimmings of piety were rarely in evidence.)

The Oxford Movement was not the first reaction against
this kind of churchmanship. First came the Methodists, then
the Evangelicals, both of whom brought passionate conviction to the practice of their religion and were therefore hope-
lessly vulgar. John Newman had been converted by an Evangelical schoolmaster, and this colored his outlook to the end of
his life.

Whereas the Evangelicals depended on a single personal
relationship between each soul and its God, each man and his
Bible, the Oxford Movement looked for the shape and authority of the Church. It looked backward down the years
toward the Reformation and beyond the Reformation to the
earliest ages of Christianity. Its members did not want to go
over to Rome, with all its corruptions. But they longed for the
traditions of the early Church, for the ages of faith, and above
all for *authority*. Newman, studying ever deeper into the history of the early Church, the writings of the fathers, more
and more longed for some authority to guide the footsteps of
theology. The English Church allowed too much personal
freedom. The Roman Church allowed too little. Authority
and discipline of some kind, however, one must have. And the
Via Media, the *middle way,* was born.

So the Oxford Movement was two contradictory things:
a movement of reform which yet looked backward rather than
forward. And in the course of its search backward through
time to find the true and unchanging Catholic traditions

(Catholic, as opposed to *Roman* Catholic), it found many things that seemed at the time both un-English and un-Protestant. Saints' days, and the practice of fasting, and admiration for the monastic life; flowers on the altar, the wearing of vestments, respect paid to the Virgin Mary, the use of a crucifix, religious pictures, the more elaborate Gothic type of church architecture, incense. (Horrified cries of "Popery!") These, one might say, were only the trimmings of religion, but it is always the trimmings, which are easy to see and recognize, about which people feel passion.

"A set of damnable and detestable heretics," bawled one newspaper, "lately sprung up at Oxford; a sect which evidently affects Popery, and merits the heartiest condemnation of all true Christians."

And in this sort of atmosphere all sorts of dark stories circulated. The best-remembered, because it was so improbable, was about Dr. Pusey, that rather sad, stout, gentle man, from whom his son could remember nothing fiercer than once having his ear pulled for reading a novel on Sunday. "Oh, Phil, you heathen!" he said.

Dr. Pusey was traveling by coach one day when a lady passenger started talking in low and thrilling tones about the wickedness of the Movement. She knew for a solemn fact, she said, that one of its leaders was a certain Pusey and (pause for full effect) he *sacrificed a lamb* every Friday.

"Madam," said the poor man, leaning forward earnestly, "I am Dr. Pusey, and I assure you that I would not have the faintest idea how to kill a lamb."

But no doubt the good lady took that to be the kind of lie one would expect from a papistical villain, and went on spreading the tale.

8

The Parting of Friends

September 22, 1843

A Monday evening in early autumn; clumps of Michaelmas daisies in cottage gardens, the smell of wood smoke, and leaves turning yellow. A time of year when people who match their moods to the seasons feel a melancholy sense that the year is dying and once again they have failed to catch the best of it until too late.

Up at Littlemore village, three miles out of Oxford, a crowd of Oxford men, a cross-section of the university from professors to undergraduates, has gathered to hear another sermon in a different church. It will be, as they have guessed, John Henry Newman's last sermon preached in the Church of England, and the thought of the future is weighing heavily on all of them.

As they walked up Iffley Hill toward Littlemore, it was almost automatic to turn around for that famous view of Oxford in the distance, its spires and towers caught by the sun or gleaming in the rain. It was a view that John had looked at almost every day for years, and always it was full of meaning, now more than ever.

"Each college, each church—he counted them by their pinnacles and turrets." (*Loss and Gain* is called a novel, but much of it is autobiography.) "The silver Isis, the grey willows, the far-stretching plains, the dark groves, the distant range of Shotover, the pleasant village where he had lived . . . wood, water, stone, all so calm, so bright, they might have been his, but his they were not. Whatever he was to gain by becoming a Catholic, this he had lost. . . . He could not have another Oxford, he could not have the friends of his boyhood and youth in the choice of his manhood."

He is still Vicar of St. Mary's, but he no longer preaches there. For some time past he has not felt happy about using this sounding board for his unorthodox views: "Is it right to be preaching to those who are not in any sense my charge, and whose legitimate guardians, the Heads of Houses, wish them not preached to?"

So a curate of more orthodox views takes St. Mary's, and Newman has moved entirely to the chapel-of-ease which goes with the parish, Littlemore.

And now at last, this September, he cannot in honesty go on any longer as a working priest within the Church of England. He has resigned his living, and this Monday evening service marks a step which many have feared for long and from which, once taken, there will be no going back. Apprehension is heavy. If they lose Newman, what will happen to the whole Church of England? He will undoubtedly take with him into the wilderness a crowd of his followers, for one reason or another (the landslide, in fact, has begun already), and what then will be left?

"How vividly comes back the remembrance," one of them wrote twenty-five years later, "of the aching blank, the awful pause which fell on Oxford when that voice had ceased, and we knew we should hear it no more. It was as when, to one kneeling by night, in the silence of some vast cathedral, the great bell tolling solemnly overhead was suddenly gone still."

This day and this service mark the seventh anniversary of the consecration of Littlemore Church, and Littlemore meant very much to Newman and to the whole Oxford Movement.

The village is not at all handsome. Then it was a scatter of poor cottages without a single good house; you can still drive through without really noticing that it is there, and if you did not know that the church ought to be looked at, there would be no reason for a backward glance. It stands by the road, a plain building with narrow lancet windows, rather a chapel than a church, you might well think. It does not seem likely that people wrote to Newman from all over the country, as they did, enthusiastically asking for the plans to copy.

The point was that this church, perhaps the first in England since the Reformation, was in the Gothic style, and so was linked, a practical symbol in stone, with all that the Oxford Movement stood for. Very plain early Gothic, to be sure, nothing like the elaboration that flourished later, at the height of the Gothic revival, when even railway stations looked like enchanted castles from a German fairy tale. But in 1836, to return to the twelfth century for the inspiration of a new church was to ally one's thinking with the Catholic middle ages in an unmistakable way.

For seven years Littlemore had been a joy and a refuge. It had been a place where things got done, practical things. It was remote from fierce argument. The children were taught, the poor had the gospel preached to them, a nice little church was built; the village people did not see further than that. Parson no doubt had some of the peculiarities proper to the gentry, but his kindness made their bald lives a little more interesting, and they didn't mind obliging him by attending church in return. Just three miles out of Oxford, but it is doubtful whether they had heard of the Oxford Movement and the rows that crashed and rumbled around it. Probably they heard no whisper even of the worst storm of all, four years old now but still growling on the horizon.

Out of the flood of Newman's books, tracts, sermons, pamphlets, the one that really blew up in his face was simply known as Tract 90. He was always shortsighted when it came to judging the effects of his actions on other people. He was astonished, genuinely astonished (so was Keble, who had passed the draft manuscript as "very likely to answer the purpose") to find that he had stepped on a land mine.

Briefly, the point of Tract 90 was this: to prove that the Thirty-nine Articles of the Church of England, the Reformers' cornerstone or sea wall, could in fact be interpreted to lie comfortably in the same bed with the Catholic doctrines that they had originally been intended to defeat.

This called for a fairly gymnastic mind, as a few examples will show. For instance:

> Article 22. Of Purgatory. The Romish Doctrine concerning Purgatory, Pardons, Worshipping and Adoration, as well of Images as of Reliques, and also invocation of Saints, is a fond thing vainly invented, and grounded upon no warranty of Scripture, but rather repugnant to the Word of God.
>
> Article 25. Of the Sacraments. . . . There are two Sacraments ordained of Christ our Lord in the Gospel, that is to say,

Baptism, and the Supper of the Lord. Those five commonly called Sacraments, that is to say, Confirmation, Penance, Orders, Matrimony, and extreme Unction, are not to be counted for Sacraments of the Gospel.

Article 28. Of the Lord's Supper. . . . Transubstantiation (or the change of the substance of Bread and Wine) in the Supper of the Lord, cannot be proved by Holy Writ; but is repugnant to the plain words of Scripture. . . . The Body of Christ is given, taken, and eaten, in the Supper, only after an heavenly and spiritual manner.

Granted that human language is a poor vehicle for theology, one can see quite easily that to reconcile these apparently straightforward statements with their apparently straightforward opposites was bound to lead to trouble for the man who tried it. ("Popery!" "Jesuits!" "Roman spies!" "Turn him out of Oxford!")

Newman's comment, "I have got into what may prove a serious mess," seems the understatement of the year. However, the uproar died down, he got away with no worse punishment than a condemnation from the Heads of Houses. "Posted up by the Marshall on the buttery hatch of every college of my University after the manner of discommoned pastry-cooks," said Newman bitterly, but one is tempted to ask, what on earth did he expect?

Thereafter, however, he began to retire from the front line, afraid that his influence was driving people into the Church of Rome. As yet he had no conscious intention of going over there himself. ("From the end of 1841 I was on my death-bed, as regards my membership with the Anglican Church, though at the time I became aware of it only by degrees.")

Littlemore was a refuge. He could restring his old violin and use it to teach the children how to sing Gregorian chant for the Sunday service. He could teach his Sunday school, though even here his fame spread and there was often an audience of Oxford scholars to hear the children chanting in chorus the names of the nine choirs of angels. On feast days he could decorate his altar with bunches of wild flowers—even this innocent prettiness smelled to some of popery. Jemima made him a beautiful embroidered altar cloth.

"Easter Eve, 8 p.m. . . . We went to church, and with much care arranged the altar cloth, covering it all over afterwards. It looks beautiful, and B. is quite in ecstasies about it. . . . Indeed, we are all so happy that we are afraid of being too happy. We have got some roses, wall-flowers, and sweetbriar, and the Chapel smells as if to remind one of the Holy Sepulchre."

("Afraid of being too happy." Not much danger of that, given his particular temperament, but it is a Newmanish phrase.)

Oxford getting really too hot to hold him, he finally moved to Littlemore altogether; carting his library out there was quite a problem. He had ideas of founding the first English monastery since the Reformation, but events moved too fast for him. He bought the land and planted trees, but by the time they were grown into saplings he and his friends were far away.

As a preliminary canter, however, he did acquire a range of old stables, which, reconditioned, made something like a row of almshouses, their backs to the highroad, their doors giving on an open-sided roof, a kind of cloister. The barn at the end of the row was a convenient library.

It was not a grand building, but it worked. Here he lived for some time, and others came and joined him when they liked, for as long as they liked. (Ironically, fathers sent their sons whose ideas were tending too much toward Rome, for Newman to "calm them down.")

People came and went for a few days, for a month, for several months. They lived under rules, rising at five, breakfasting at half past six, spending most of the day in silence, study, and prayer. A village woman came in to cook the dinner, her son cleaned the boots—a nice Victorian touch, this: one might live under the strictest discipline, even to sleeping on the bare floor, but a boy came in to clean the boots.

Knowing the end of the story, as we do, it seems I suppose inevitable that he would end up in the Roman Catholic Church. Both then and now, there were plenty of people who felt, and feel, nothing but impatience. What held him back? Why did he take so long? Was he really honest in hanging about, protesting that he intended no change?

It is so much easier to see things by hindsight. Both Pusey and Keble remained inside the Church of England, though Pusey was suspended from preaching for several years. The uproar died down, and both of them lived to be loved and honored inside the Anglican Church. You cannot help wondering why Newman finally went, what it was that would have kept him inside too. It was certainly not a temperamental attraction that drew him to Rome. He hated the idea and quite late in the day wrote down in a list of "various great trials" which might happen to him: "Having to join the Church of Rome."

"I cannot make out that I have any motive but indefinite risk to my own soul in remaining where I am. A clear con-

viction of the substantial identity of Christianity and the
Roman system has now been on my mind for a full three
years. It is more than five years since the conviction first came
on me, though I struggled against it and overcame it. I believe all my feelings and wishes are against change. I have
nothing to draw me elsewhere. I hardly ever was at a Roman
service, even abroad—I know no Roman Catholics. I have no
sympathy with them as a party. I am giving up everything. I
am not conscious of any resentment, disgust, or the like, to
repel me from my present position; and I have no dreams
whatsoever, far from it, of what I could do in another position.
Far from it—I seem to be throwing myself away."

And now that the background is sketched in, we can see
why, on that September evening in 1843 (though still he
hesitated, and it would be eighteen months before the final
crossing), the sense of doom was heavy, the feeling of "throwing himself away" hung like a cloud in Littlemore Church,
where next Sunday a new vicar would take the service.

It needs an effort of imagination to feel the temper of the
times, when such a step seemed so terrible. Henry Wilberforce was gloomily there, who had said, "I do feel it would
give me less pain to hear of your death than of your leaving
the church of your baptism." Pusey, conducting the service,
confessed afterward to having done so in tears.

Newman had a feeling for symbols. He preached from
the text "Man goeth forth to his work and to his labor until
the evening." It had been the text of his first sermon, and
afterwards he had shut himself up in his Oriel room and
thrown himself on the sofa, wriggling with embarrassment to
think what a fool he had made of himself.

Things were different now, apart from the fact that he

no longer suffered agonies at the sound of his own voice. Then it had been all about the "going forth"; now it was the evening. In its printed version, the sermon is called *The Parting of Friends*. There is something particularly moving about public words which can be taken to refer to private feelings, and as the familiar voice referred to all the leave-takings of the Old and New Testaments, speaking as everyone had always heard him speak, low, in little rushes, with long pauses between, each person who heard it suffered more because they read the underlying meaning than if the meaning had been openly stated.

He appealed to the Church of England: "O mother of saints! O school of the wise! O nurse of the heroic! . . . O thou, from whom surrounding nations lit their lamps!" But it seemed as though the lamps were going out. The Church had fallen upon such evil days that she could not keep or use the work of those who loved her best. "Why hast thou not the skill to use their services, nor the heart to rejoice in their love?" He spoke not only for himself. Pusey was proscribed from teaching; the first of the Littlemore men had just gone over to Rome, a grave shock; Tom Mozley, Harriet's husband, had with difficulty been persuaded to wait for a while. Every word the preacher spoke meant something personal and painful to his congregation.

There was not a breath in the crowded church as he reached his final paragraph. Still, Newmanlike, he could not bring himself to be personal, to pronounce the direct goodbye.

"And, O my brethren, O kind and affectionate hearts, O loving friends, should you know any one whose lot it has been, by writing, or by word of mouth, in some degree to help you. . . . If he has ever told you what you knew about yourselves, or what you did not know; has read to you your wants or feelings, and comforted you by the very reading; has made you feel that there was a higher life than this daily one, and a brighter world than that you see; or encouraged you, or sobered you, or opened a way to the enquiring, or soothed the perplexed; if what he has said or done has ever made you take an interest in him, and feel well inclined towards him; remember such a one in time to come, though you hear him not, and pray for him, that in all things he may know God's Will, and at all times he may be ready to fulfil it."

Then he left the altar, and as he went, consciously or not, he took off his gown, the mark of his Oxford scholarship and his belonging to the Church, and threw it over the altar rails. If the change was not yet complete, everyone present knew it to be inevitable.

One could end this chapter with the screaming outburst of rage, grief, disappointment, contempt that followed his defection. It is comforting to know that the best of his friends were able to ride the storm. Keble spoke no reproaches to Newman, though he had some for himself.

> I keep on thinking, "If I had been different, perhaps Newman would have been guided to see things differently, and we might have been spared so many broken hearts and bewildered spirits.". . .
>
> My dearest Newman, you have been a kind and helpful friend to me in a way in which scarce anyone else could have been, and you are so mixed up in my mind with old and dear and sacred thoughts that I cannot well bear to part with you, most unworthy as I know myself to be. And yet I cannot go along with you. I must cling to the belief that we are not really parted:

you have taught me so, and I scarce think you can un-teach me. . . .

May you have peace where you are gone, and help us in some way to get peace; but somehow I scarce think it will be in the way of controversy. And so, with some-what of a feeling as if the spring had been taken out of my year,

I am, always, your affectionate and grateful,
J. Keble.

9

Into the Desert

And then what happened? Just when the story seems about to break into a fanfare of trumpets—either a spectacular end or a spectacular beginning, the breaking of a Technicolor dawn or the closing of a Technicolor sunset . . . nothing.

John Henry Newman disappeared like a man walking into a desert. It would be hard to know who was the more relieved, the English Church that survived the shock of his going, or the Roman Church that survived the shock of his arrival.

It had seemed a real danger that with Newman's defection the Anglican Church would crumble. It did indeed rock as wave after wave of the brightest and best young minds went off after him. (One hundred and thirty clergymen, some hundreds of lay people, in the next ten years.) But when the first excitement was over, things were not so very bad. The old Church was more solidly built than had been suspected, and it was still standing. Some of the best minds had left, but others had stayed. And some who went were no great loss; there were a number of unstable characters, persuaded by the glamour of their leader rather than by their own judgment; others, as always, went for security—to be told what to think and to escape the burden of making up their own minds.

Of course, some stayed for motives that were not quite the best. The author's great-grandfather had it squarely put before him by his father that if he changed his religion he would be disinherited. A considerable estate was involved; the young man thought twice and remained a pillar of the Church of England to the day of his death. His sister, with more spirit, or fewer expectations, made the change with her husband and children, and the resulting bitter split in the family took eighty years to heal. This shows well enough the kind of atmosphere people breathed at the time.

What about the view from the Roman Catholic side of the fence? If the Church of England rocked as he went out of the door, it was likely that the Church of Rome (at least that part of it in England) would rock just as violently as he went in. No man of that size, in brain and character, had been seen among them since the Reformation.

The English Catholics constituted a tiny, downtrodden, ghetto church, not much swelled as yet by Irish immigration except in one or two big cities. In the north there was still a strong working-class element. Up there, in the remoter counties, the stamping-out process of the sixteenth century had been much less successful than in the south. But on the whole, Catholic society was heavily weighted on the aristocratic side, with the Duke of Norfolk and all the Howard family at the top of the list. At one time it had been a very expensive business to remain a Catholic, and it was only the proudest, most obstinate, and best-heeled families who had been able to manage it. They remained a silent, conservative group, keeping themselves to themselves, much intermarried, poorly educated (they had no proper public school for their sons, and the universities were closed to them), living quietly behind high walls and marrying their own second cousins.

It was this Church and this society that accepted, if accept is not too strong a word, John Henry Newman in 1845. Before his conversion, he said that he did not know any Roman Catholics personally and did not like what he saw of them. He walked with his eyes open into the desert: "going out on the open sea" was his own phrase.

One feels a shock to catch up with him in 1863, nearly twenty years later: a thin, gray-haired man with a face permanently furrowed by nervous strain. Gone is the scholarly elegance of Oxford, and instead we are in the gray Midlands, the city of Birmingham, an industrial town that could not be suspected of having much to do with things of the mind. He is still surrounded by books and pictures and, of course, still writing. He has always been a great one for writing things down to clear his mind, sometimes in a daily journal, sometimes a kind of summing up that goes into a different book. On this date he writes, in a little exercise book with marbled covers, a summary of what he feels he has gained by twenty years of struggling not to "sin against the light," and it makes sad reading.

"This morning, when I woke, the feeling that I was cumbering the ground came on me so strongly that I could not get myself to go to my shower bath. I said, what is the good of trying to preserve or increase strength, when nothing comes of it? What is the good of living for nothing? . . .

"How forlorn and dreary has been my course since I have been a Catholic! Here has been the contrast—as a Protestant, I felt my religion dreary, but not my life—but, as a

Catholic, my life dreary, not my religion. Of course one's early years are (humanly speaking) best, and again events are softened by distance—and I look back on my years at Oxford and Littlemore with tenderness. And it was the time when I had a remarkable mission—but how am I changed even in look. Till the affair of No. 90 and my going to Littlemore, I had my mouth half open, and commonly a smile on my face, and, from that time onwards my mouth has been closed and contracted, and the muscles are so set now, that I cannot but look grave and forbidding. Even as early as 1847, when I was going through the Vatican with Dalgairns, stopping before a statue of Fate which was very striking and stern and melancholy, he said: 'Who *can* it be like? I know the face so well!' Presently he added: 'Why, it is you!' "

Everybody noticed how the years of dreariness had marked him. An old friend visited him and wrote:

"I shall never forget, nor could I ever describe, the brightness that lit up that worn face as he received me at the door, carrying in several packages himself. . . . When the hurry of the arrival, necessary arrangements, etc., were over and we were talking in the Guest Room I saw for the first time a great change in Fr. Newman. He had not only aged disproportionately to the time but his grand massive face was scored with lines which no lapse of years had written there. They were too evidently lines of intense grief, disappointment and the patient bearing up against the failure of hope. Whenever he spoke the expression softened, but when at rest, and his conversation was frequently broken short by fits of absence, there was even a look of terrible weariness akin to lasting depression of mind."

It is the picture of a man apparently broken. Each of us

is the sum of his experience and his temperament working on each other, and both of them working on the world with which we come in contact. In this sense we create our own lives continuously. Nothing in John Henry Newman's life suggests that he would ever have found things easy, whatever the external circumstances. There was a sense in which "dreariness" was built-in for him. His make-up was a bundle of qualities which made the stony desert inevitable but which enabled him at the same time to cross it and come out on the other side, not less of a person, but more, against the odds.

His very qualities worked against him, for they were also his defects. To be extremely sensitive may be the sign of a fine spirit, but it is a quality that leads to trouble; for ordinary workaday uses, a somewhat thick skin has its advantages. His honesty was too acute, following every twist and wriggle of his own mind, so that it could be mistaken for deviousness. The very brilliant mind attracted people and also frightened them. He had, to his suffering, a temperament that misjudged and mistrusted others, sometimes could not see them at all for his own self in the foreground. His presence seemed to make demands, it switched on a searchlight that revealed people to themselves, and not all of them could stand this. Enthusiastic followers had said: "The heroic was a kind of natural element with him." "It was like God speaking to you." "He spoke with such piercing insight that you thought the secrets of your own heart had been revealed to him." Inspiring when you were in the mood to be inspired—but how singularly uncomfortable if you were not! Such qualities arouse as much repulsion as attraction. It was almost impossible to be neutral about such a man. Either you followed willingly—sometimes blindly, to his great embarrassment—or you reacted against him and in reacting had to find reasons to prove yourself right. The waters around him were never calm.

What, in fact, had happened during these twenty years to bring him to the all-time low of January 21, 1863, when he wrote in his journal: "What am I living for?"

At his coming into the Roman Church he was, of course, a seven-day wonder: "some wild incomprehensible beast, caught by the hunter, and a spectacle for Dr. Wiseman to exhibit to strangers, as himself being the hunter who captured it! I did not realize this at the time except in discomfort."

He behaved with dignity, tried to efface himself and waited to be told what to do next, but Newman being self-effacing was even more noticeable than Newman expressing himself. The dignitaries of the Catholic Church could not help feeling that they had in their hands a very hot potato.

He went to Rome with Ambrose St. John, the last of his friends, a kindly, warm, faithful sheepdog of a man who hardly left Newman's side until death (the wrong death—it was Ambrose, the younger by fifteen years, who died first). Some of the other Littlemore converts went too.

They were received by the Pope, given medals and pictures, but not given any work to do, except one small task, the wrong task, which blotted Newman's copybook more thoroughly than anything he ever did in his life. He was asked to preach a funeral sermon for an Englishwoman, and for whatever reason, in front of all the English society in Rome (most of it not Catholic), himself not so much as a deacon as yet, he preached a highhanded sermon telling them where, as heretics, they got off. (This has embarrassed everybody so much that no one seems to have kept a copy of what he actually said, but it is easy enough to know the effect it had). The congregation was furious. It was not out of character that at a really difficult moment he should misjudge the temper of other people, but the punishment was too heavy. For years it was remembered against him—some people seem never to have remembered anything else.

That was, one might say, a small thing, and there was plenty of positive work to do. Newman and his group were to be ordained priests. What was to be done with them? They did not want to part, they had lived at Littlemore together in what amounted to a religious life. But how? Benedictine? Jesuit? Dominican? None seemed quite right. Newman himself found the answer almost by accident. An oratory.

The Oratory of St. Philip Neri was not an order. It was a loose association of men living together, keeping their own possessions, without vows, but under a common rule. The organization was much slighter and more democratic than that of the monastic orders, but because it seemed easier it was in some ways more difficult; they had to learn to keep to a spirit without many letters of the law to help.

This just suited John Henry—he could not avoid being the founder and superior of whatever group he set up, but he did not like giving orders and preferred things to grow of themselves. The idea of priests living together but each following his own line—in parish work, or in study, or in schools —seemed just right for nineteenth-century England. Perhaps they could look ahead to an oratory in every big industrial town: Manchester, Newcastle, Bristol, Sheffield. The first was started in Birmingham.

There was scope for trouble, and trouble came very quickly. Two oratories were founded: one in Birmingham on purpose, and a second in London almost by accident, to take the men who could not, or would not, live under Newman. Difficulties, flaring into quarrels, split the congregation and astonished the onlookers. The letters they sent each other almost blistered the pages; never, it seems, have people misunderstood one another so badly and so continuously.

Worse, it was the London Oratory, separated at last, which flourished, and Birmingham which seemed to shrivel. Father Faber in London (read some of the more flowery of his hymns and you get the flavor of his religion) was a thoroughly Italian Catholic. The converts, going to Rome, had brought back everything but the kitchen stove—rituals, customs, sentimental art. It went down well in Victorian middle-class England, and flocks of new converts came to the papal flag in Brompton. Later they built a very ornate Italian church that is still unlike anything else in London.

At the same time the Birmingham Oratory seemed hardly to be getting off the ground. Some of its members left, and there were few new converts except among the working class. Birmingham was a backwater. Newman was suspected of sulking. No further oratories were founded.

Still, nobody used the best brain in England. Then someone thought of sending him to Ireland to found a Catholic university. Hope bloomed again. This was a dream after his own heart. Why should not all the Catholics of the English-speaking world, in time, send their sons to get an education that would take the best of both worlds: the intellectual and the religious?

For several years Newman commuted between Birmingham and Dublin, working like a maniac. But it was hitting his head against a brick wall. He was too liberal for the Irish Church authorities, and he did not understand their politics.

They liked him personally, but they did not want the kind of university he wanted. They wanted a kind of enlarged seminary to train laymen who would know their place and keep to it.

Nor did he get the support from Cardinal Archbishop Wiseman that he might have expected. At one moment Wiseman decided that if Newman were made a bishop he would have the authority he needed to deal with the Irish. Wiseman announced this move to Newman, and announced it to the rest of the country, before it was confirmed from Rome. Congratulations came by every post, and letters addressing Newman as "My Lord," and handsome presents. Someone sent an episcopal cross. And then silence. Nothing happened. Someone, somewhere in the winding passages of the Roman establishment, had worked against him all too successfully. It was a shaming humiliation for anyone—to a temperament like Newman's it must have been nearly fatal.

He struggled against the odds in Dublin for four years, and in the end gave up, leaving nothing behind him but one of his best-known books, *The Idea of a University.*

Other things happened, failed to happen. Everything Newman touched seemed blighted because he touched it.

"Persons who would naturally look towards me, converts who would naturally come to me, inquirers who would naturally consult me," he burst out in one of his bitterest moments, "are stopped by some light or unkind words said against me. I am *passé*, in decay; I am untrustworthy; I am strange, odd; I have my own ways and cannot get on with others; something or other is said in disparagement. I am put aside on the ground that I ought to be put aside; and thus men make statements of which their very words bring about the fulfilment. Nor is it wonderful that all this slight and scorn reacts upon my own mind. I shrink from a society which is so unjust towards me."

There were many stories to the effect that he wanted to change back again, even that he *had* changed back again, or under the double blow lost all faith.

"What has become of the great giant of intellect and sanity—John Henry Newman?" asked a newspaper article. "I have the authority of a clergyman of high church caste . . . for saying that he has become utterly *sceptical*."

He had not. He did not regret his step, if regret means wishing it untaken, although he referred to his conversion as the "great sacrifice to which God called me."

One more extract from a letter to a friend, at this same time of lost hopes. "To myself I feel as full of thought and life as ever I was, but a certain invisible chain impedes me, or bar stops me, when I attempt to do anything—and the only reason why I do not *enjoy* the happiness of being out of the conflict is, because I feel to myself I could do much in it. But in fact I could not do much in it. I should come into collision with everyone I met—I should be treading on everyone's toes."

There is a movement to have John Henry Newman canonized. If it succeeds, perhaps he will be made the patron of all the sad souls who carry the weight of the modern world —the neurotic, the overintroverted, the outsiders, the non-communicators, all those who are overweighted with intellect to the loss of affection. None of these are crimes. A man can be a saint carrying such a load as that. But he has a particularly steep road to climb.

10

Apologia pro Vita Sua

May 20, 1864

John Henry Newman, the old tired priest in his black habit
with the funny little white turned-down collar which is the
mark of the Oratory: he sits at his desk writing, and the whole
room is tumbled with letters and papers and books with slips
of paper to mark a special place. Opposite on the wall hangs a
large sheet of paper to which he sometimes refers, with chapter, subject, paragraph headings in a tangle of cross references.

He works steadily through the day and into the evening,
eating a sandwich absently with one hand when someone
brings it to him at dinnertime; the someone almost certainly
Ambrose St. John, himself now elderly and asthmatic and de-
cidedly round-bellied, but still Newman's best friend and self-
appointed nursemaid. The writer writes on, and stops, stuck
over a sentence or a word. He gets up and paces the floor
between the heaps of overflowing papers, or stands by the
window, flexing a tired wrist and looking out on the Birmingham darkness. Then he goes back to the desk as the clock
strikes still another relentless hour, and suddenly tears up a

sheaf of manuscript and throws it away, pulling out a clean sheet and starting again in a fine scholarly hand that wriggles ever more unreadably as he gets more and more tired.

"As if I were ploughing in very stiff clay," he said afterward, and anyone who has ever tried to write must sympathize with the description. "It was moving on at the rate of a mile an hour, when I had to write and print and correct a hundred miles by the next day's post. . . . The longest book I ever wrote, in ten weeks, without any preparation or anticipation, and not only written, but printed and corrected. . . ."

There was no time to stop. The man from the publishers' came promptly every Thursday morning, and the week's stint had to be finished. Finished each time it was, on several occasions after sixteen hours, once after a solid stretch of twenty-two hours. In print the book runs to more than three hundred close pages, and each of them, in Newman's way, was hand-written and rewritten and overwritten and better written until, although not satisfied, he knew he could do no more, or until Thursday came around again, and the knock on the door, and the installment had to be hastily parceled and sent off just as it was.

It was a tremendous physical achievement, as well as an intellectual one. He ought to have ended his ten weeks' stretch in a state of nervous collapse, but in fact he didn't.

For this was the swing of the pendulum that always carried John Henry from depths to heights and back again, in a series of slow arcs throughout his life. This time he was on the upgrade and the years rolled off his back.

The series of pamphlets, published at two shillings each, are collected now under the title *Apologia pro Vita Sua*, which cannot be simply translated. There is nothing apologetic about the Greek-Latin word, rather the opposite.

It was an autobiography, and yet not a simple one written more or less at random. It was nothing less than a reasoned explanation of who he was and what he was and why he found himself, in 1864, inside the Church of Rome instead of the Church of England. It was the whole history of his religious life, as well as he could set it down, step by step. To get that into brown paper covers within two months—this explains the white heat of his working.

But the *Apologia* is not famous for the speed at which it was written, which is interesting but irrelevant. It remains one of the very great spiritual autobiographies. At that time, with the interest in theology and churchmanship, and the morbid fascination of the Church of Rome, it was a bestseller. When only two weekly numbers were out, it was reported from Oxford, "men are carrying those brown pamphlets in their hands, reading them as they go along." Traffic problems were less acute in those days.

At the beginning of the year, Newman had been in as low water as he was ever to be in his life, forgotten by the ordinary world, forgotten by most of his old Oxford friends (though one or two made tentative approaches; they heard rumors that he was badly treated by his new church, and could not help hoping that it was time to send him friendly word from the old one).

The Catholic Establishment, both in England and in Rome, mistrusted him. He was not quite sound. It was even said: "Dr. Newman is the most dangerous man in England." His chief opponent was Manning, soon to be Archbishop of Westminster. The old Archbishop, Wiseman, had not liked or trusted Newman much; the new one, though himself an Oxford convert, would like and trust him even less. He was suspected of being too liberal, too protestant, even a little bit heretical. He had written an article about which Rome had demanded an explanation that it never got, because it went to them in Manning's pocket and stayed there. Newman did not find out that the explanation was not delivered, he merely sensed a coldness in official circles, and he knew for a fact that he was left to eat his heart out in Birmingham, like the best regiment left behind with the stores while the battle rages up ahead.

Then, in January 1864, someone sent him a cutting from a magazine. In a book review he was mentioned by name, casually, the book itself having nothing to do with him.

"Truth, for its own sake, had never been a virtue with the Roman clergy. Father Newman informs us that it need not, and on the whole ought not to be; that cunning is the weapon which Heaven has given to the saints wherewith to withstand the brute male force of the wicked world which marries and is given in marriage." The review was signed with the initials C.K.

Newman said afterward that he did not realize that C.K. stood for Charles Kingsley. It was not an unusual attack from some circles, and there were plenty of other people who might have written it, but it is in fact typical Kingsley. Most people know him now perhaps as the author of that curious children's book *The Water Babies,* but at the time he was well known also as a writer of novels, some of them rather good novels but running to a pattern in their presentation of villainy; nearly all the villains are nasty Roman Catholic foreigners or, worse, Roman priests.

If you read his life, you find that Kingsley in fact was an attractive, though exasperating man, blissfully happy with wife and children, interested in putting right the social wrongs of his time—hearty, normal, commonsensical to a degree; "muscular Christianity," his kind of religion was nicknamed.

"A way of talking," somebody said, "with the air and spirit of a man bouncing up from the table with his mouth full of bread and cheese and saying that he meant to stand no blasted nonsense. There is a whole volume of Kingsley's essays which is all a munch and a not standing of any blasted nonsense from cover to cover."

He was Regius Professor of Modern History at Cambridge, but not a real scholar. . . . "Mr. Kingsley, in the ordinary steeplechase fashion in which he chooses not so much to think as to *splash* up thought—dregs and all—(often very healthy and sometimes very noble, but always very loose thought) in one's face." It sums him up very neatly.

If there was one thing that roused him to almost hysterical horror, it was nonmarriage, deliberate nonmarriage. He must have accepted the other kind easily enough, for Victorian middle-class life was full of unmarried women, the patient aunts of every household. But deliberate nonmarriage —the sight of a nunnery, or the thought of celibate priests— this roused him to roaring. One can see that the figure of Newman was just the one to make him see red—the quiet, withdrawn figure, the low voice, the rather feminine gliding walk, the preoccupation with mind rather than matter, the severely disciplined priestly life. Kingsley had heard Newman preach years before, as an undergraduate, and had been impressed, very impressed. It was partly because he felt that he had escaped by the skin of his teeth that Newman made him so mad now.

So, it is not just a stupidly rude remark in a book review that we have to consider. It is a clash of opposites drawn together by contradiction.

Kingsley wrote his review. Newman wrote to the publishers, pointing out that they would hardly care to be associated with such an offensive lie. The publishers contacted Kingsley, who answered, offering to apologize but making the apology sound like a further attack. Newman pointed this out. Kingsley toned down his words, though he still did not sound very apologetic. Macmillan's printed the apology, and that ought to have been the end of that.

It was not. Given the two men, and the situation, the matter would not be suffered to rest. "I have a score of more than twenty years to pay," Kingsley said to his publisher, though he did not explain exactly what sort of a score it was. "It has always been on my mind that perhaps some day I should be called on to defend my honesty," said Newman.

Here was his chance. Here was the field cleared and the weapon put into his hand, and all the bitter disappointments of twenty years clamored for justification.

Instead of accepting the apology, Newman published all the letters on both sides, with a roaring satirical commentary at the end. Intellectually he could run rings around Kingsley. The pamphlet made people laugh, and the papers took up the fight, cheering on both sides. Said one of them, "How briskly we gather round a brace of reverend gentlemen, when the prize for which they contend is which of the two shall be considered the father of lies!"

Kingsley returned the blow with interest. *He* published

a pamphlet entitled "What, then, did Dr. Newman mean?"
It was a bold, foolish, muddled attack. Clear argument had
never been his strong point, and it vanished altogether from
the pages of prejudice that poured out of him. The original
argument was that Roman priests did not believe overmuch in
truthfulness, but it widened out, as arguments have a habit of
doing in unskillful hands, until Kingsley was making an all-
guns-firing attack on Newman: he was a liar and a hypocrite,
his whole life had been a web of lies and hypocrisy, all proved
by the fact that he had defected to Rome.

It was a heavy-handed attack, but like all complicated
attacks, which are so much more interesting than defenses, it
would be hard to answer point by point. Worse, the answer
would necessarily be dull, and nobody would read it. Newman did in fact do a point-by-point defense, but he left it to
the end. He saw that what he had to do first was to make his
public listen to him. He must explain his whole religious life,
show the steps by which he had become a Roman Catholic, and
show how they followed inevitably from the rest of his life.

His publishers said that it had to be done at once if it was
done at all: strike while the iron is hot, Mr. Newman. Newman therefore undertook to supply weekly parts for pamphlet
publication. And so began the *Apologia*.

The first two sections, demolishing Kingsley's position in
general, are cruelly effective. It is not pleasant to see anyone
being cut to pieces as completely as that, and it was indeed
the end of Kingsley's reputation as a scholar, which was never
very high. One wishes, in reading, that Newman had been
kinder; perhaps, looking back, he did too, for he left these
sections out of later editions. Then you remember the depths
his life had reached. Kingsley represented a multitude of aunt

sallies; there had not been a chance to shy at them for twenty years, and now there was. To expect *kindness* at this stage would be asking for the truly superhuman.

The important, best-selling parts of the book, those sections written at such white heat through days and nights, are quite different: calm and reasoned, yet deeply moving as he turns out his spiritual pockets, puts everything on the table. Of course, it is not a complete picture. Introspective though he was, there was very much about himself that he did not know; but he put down everything he did know. And it hurt. It hurt very much. He wanted people to know the whole story, but he was still John Henry Newman who had squirmed on the sofa after his first sermon. He shrank many times, but he gritted his teeth and went on with the job. And as he retraced the history of all those years, from time to time he cried to think how young he had been, and how happy, and sometimes how unhappy.

"You must remember," he once said to Hurrell Froude, "that every thought I think is thought, and every word I write is writing." It was still true; he was not satisfied with anything on the surface, it was all dredged up at some cost from the very bottom of himself.

In the midst of all this painful hard work, nothing was pleasanter than to see how his old friends of the Church of England rallied around him. He had to write to many of them for copies of letters, if they still kept them, which would illustrate the state of his thinking in this year or that. "Don't suppose I shall say one word unkind to the Church of England at least in my intentions," he said reassuringly, and he did not. The glow of those happy years still shone, and he wrote warmly, not only of Keble and Pusey and Bowden and Hurrell Froude, but of many others who had not understood him so well or been so loyal as they.

The Oxford Movement was still not well accepted by much of the Church of England; they still felt misunderstood and somewhat cut off, so they welcomed the *Apologia* for their own reasons. Newman had left the Church, and they had stayed, but while it showed that he had left honestly, it also showed that they had stayed honestly.

It is difficult to understand how much the publication of this book changed the climate of opinion in Newman's favor. Most people still did not think that he was right to have made the change, but at least they thought of it now as a mistake, no worse, and to be mistaken is no crime. His stock went up among fellow Catholics too. For in writing about himself he had effectively defended all of them who were converts, and particularly all who were priests.

There were plenty more battles ahead, but the low tide had been reached and passed and he need never go back again to the depths of "What am I living for? . . . What is the good of living for nothing?"

11

The Running Battle

And he was to live twenty-five years more! All that had happened, and there was still a quarter of a century to go.

Three years after the publication of the *Apologia* he wrote once more in that little exercise book where, over the years, he had every so often put down a progress report.

"I never was in such simply happy circumstances as now. . . . I am my own master—I have my time my own—I am surrounded with comforts and conveniences—I have no cares, I have good health—I have no pain of mind or body. I enjoy life only too well. The weight of years falls on me as snow, gently tho' surely, but I do not feel it yet. I am surrounded with dear friends—my reputation has been cleared by the *Apologia*. What can I want but greater love and gratitude to the Giver of all these good things? There is no state of life I prefer to my own—I would not change my position for that of anyone I know—I am simply content—there is nothing I desire. . . . I have nothing to ask for but pardon and grace, and a happy death."

The temper of the times had clearly changed. With his *Apologia,* Newman had become an Elder Statesman, a bridge

between the two Churches. Not everyone approved of him—
that would have been too much to ask. But over the years,
Oriel put up a portrait of him in their common room; so did
Trinity College. What was more, Trinity offered him the
very first Honorary Fellowship they had ever bestowed, and
he was delighted by the honor. For if it showed that the college had not forgotten him, neither had he forgotten it—a
picture of Trinity hung always in his bedroom. He went up
to Oxford for the ceremony, visited the new college called
after John Keble, saw Pusey once more, and, surprisingly,
his old tutor, Mr. Short, ninety years old and blind, but still
lively. He walked up to Littlemore and saw the place again,
but it brought neither joy nor pain. The past was the past,
and although, as old men do, he remembered vividly, he was
insulated against the past.

But through all these years when he was growing older,
more bent, the stern dark lines of his middle age ironing out
and leaving the wonderful old face that looks out of his later
portraits, it must not be supposed that everything was smooth.
If it had been, he would no longer have been John Henry
Newman. Life was not all gas and gaiters: the running battle
with the extreme Romans went on.

"Newman has never been more than half-converted,"
one of them said, which from that source was a compliment.

"Newman's conversion was the greatest calamity to the
Church in England," another is reported to have said, to
which one of Newman's supporters retorted: "Not Newman's
conversion, but the death of a woman." (Manning had been
married before his conversion, and because his wife died he
was able to become a priest.) The story may not be true, but
it sums up the two points of view.

The two battlefields, which sound at first unconnected, were the Oxford question and Papal Infallibility.

The first was an English problem. The arrival in the Church of so many educated converts had showed up the shortcomings of the old Catholic families. What was needed was a strong, well-educated laity, and men who had been to the university themselves wanted their sons to go there too.

The Dublin idea had failed, but what about Oxford? Undergraduates no longer had to subscribe to the Thirty-nine Articles, so that was no barrier. But if Catholic boys went there, would they all lose their faith? For ten years the battle raged. Ought there to be a Catholic college? If so, why not Newman for its head? Ought there to be a strong chaplaincy to look after those who went to ordinary colleges? If so, why not an Oxford oratory with Newman as its Father?

But the more liberal party had to reckon with the extremists, led by Manning, Ward the editor of the *Dublin Review,* and the English papal chamberlain in Rome, a politician called George Talbot. Newman called the three of them "the three tailors of Tooley Street," because like the mythical three tailors, who began their manifesto: "We the people of England," they couldn't and wouldn't see that they were in a minority and that there were other honestly held views to be considered. They quite genuinely thought that those who were against them were against God. And the brunt of their disapproval fell on Newman. (He was actually putting out new editions of all the books he had written as an Anglican; that proved he was not a right Catholic.)

The three tailors' point of view was that, granted *some* Catholic boys went to Oxford, their numbers should be kept down and the parents discouraged. If Newman went there, who could doubt that the numbers would soar up?

Others joined in the fight. Anglicans were not at all sure that they wanted the old warrior back in his old haunts. There might be another wave of defections to Rome. "What I aim at," he said, "is not immediate conversions, but to influence, as far as an old man can, the tone of thought in the place." Which was precisely what they were all afraid of.

The fight churned backward and forward. In the end Newman was defeated. He didn't go to Oxford, and he didn't found a college or another oratory there, and the laity were temporarily hammered back into what the extremists thought was their proper place. "What is the province of the laity? To hunt, to shoot, to entertain. These matters they understand, but to meddle in ecclesiastical matters they have no right at all."

It was quite natural that the three tailors, who were so anxious (though one of them was a layman) to keep the laity in its place, should also be in the forefront of the fight to have the Infallibility of the Pope defined as an article of faith in 1870 at the Vatican Council.

Definition is of course not the producing, like a rabbit out of a hat, of a new article of faith. It crystallizes something that on the whole has been part of the traditional teaching of the Church. That the Church is in some way infallible had always been believed, but exactly where that infallibility resided and how it was exercised was a much vaguer question and had never been properly thrashed out.

Most definitions have been produced under stress, at a time of heresy, to make quite sure that the orthodox voice of the Church was clearly heard, but the infallibility definition was produced almost out of the blue by extremists, some of whom wanted its phrasing to indicate that if the Pope said it was raining, it was no use for the faithful to look at the sky. (Manning, in a moment of excitement, wanted the Church to be defined as the incarnation of the third Person of the Trinity.) Papal infallibility was defined in the end in fairly moderate terms, though even to these some bishops could not assent; they left the session so that they did not have to vote against it.

The circumstances of the final vote were highly dramatic, and those of any party or any church who enjoyed reading the finger of God into natural phenomena had plenty of scope for their different interpretations—some of course thinking that God was angry, others that he was delighted.

Tom Mozley, as it happened, was the correspondent of the London *Times,* and he sent back a vivid description.

"The *Placets* of the Fathers struggled through the storm, while the thunder pealed above and the lighting flashed in at every window and down through the dome and every smaller cupola. . . . *Placet,* shouted his Eminence or his Grace and a loud clap of thunder followed in response." Halfway through the proceedings there was a crash louder than before, followed by the tinkling of broken glass as the panes of a window were blown out almost over the Pope's head. The darkness gathered thicker and thicker, until the assembled bishops could hardly see one another's faces, and when the results of the voting were brought up to the papal throne, a fat candle had to be brought too, so he could see the words that were written.

Tom Mozley and his shorthand pad were in the south transept. He scribbled and peered through the gloom, and suddenly the noise of the storm sharpened into an indescribable rushing and pattering, as though the roof had come off and the hail were falling on the stone floor. But it was not hail—it was the clapping of hands. The thunder died away, unnoticed, drowned by the clapping that spread from the assembled bishops to the great crowds, and then the shouting began: *"Viva il Papa Infallibile!"* In a wave of emotion the whole of St. Peter's fell on its knees to receive the papal blessing.

Whatever the welcome given to the definition at that moment and in that place, the results were less happy elsewhere. "You are going too fast, you are going too fast," Newman had said, and Catholics in a number of countries left the Church because they could not cope with the sudden demand made on them. Many writers point out that the moderate phrasing of the definition was much nearer to Newman's opinion than to Manning's, but even so, there is no doubt that it was an untimely move altogether—"a great calamity," Newman called it. The results have been felt ever since.

Now that this generation has seen a Council at work, we are better equipped to understand how these things are done and how the Church can move only through its human members. ("The Church moves as a whole; it is not a mere philosophy, it is a communion," said Newman.) There are no white doves descending into St. Peter's through a hole in the roof with a whispered infallible message, but a great crowd of human men with all their human equipment of intellect, temperament, background, nationality, using all the human arts of knowledge, communication, and every sort of persuasion, some of it praiseworthy, some not.

"Truth, simple English truth, seems to have departed

from the whole faction," wrote one outraged bishop from Rome during the 1870 Council. "Nothing ever wounded the simplicity of my faith so much as the trickery with which I became acquainted on my official intercourse with the Curia."

Leave the summing-up to Newman: "As little as possible was passed at the Council—nothing about the Pope which I have not myself always held. But it is impossible to deny that it was done with an imperiousness and overbearing wilfulness which has been a great scandal—and I cannot think thunder and lightning a mark of approbation, as some persons wish to make out."

After 1870 there were still some troubles, difficulties, disapproving noises from high places, but now Newman was able to ride them, and his road eased out toward a serene old age. There are many pleasant stories which show—what all the late photographs show too—that the corners were rubbed and smoothed down until his most notable quality was a great gentleness.

A little boy whose extremely Evangelical family lived near the Oratory in Birmingham knew of John Henry Newman as "that misguided and misguiding man." Charlie used to peer out the window at the old man passing on his walk, because there was a fascination about someone who was so certainly going to hell. He didn't look like a terrible sinner, "with his keen old saintly face poking peakedly out of his comforter, a book under his arm and a loose coat on his back." (Newman had never been a dressy person in his best days, and the impression now given was of extreme shabbiness, sometimes respectable, sometimes not—he was once turned out of St. Paul's Cathedral for loitering.) Young Charles one day went down to the market and bought a guinea pig to add to his family of guinea pigs. The creature was in a brown paper bag and Charlie walked very carefully. He always walked carefully, because he had it well rubbed home that "Satan goeth about like a roaring lion, seeking whom he may devour," and if Satan was going to spring on him, it was quite possible that he might devour the guinea pig as well. There was also a more immediate danger: rough street boys who pounced on tidy boys and jeered at them, stole their caps, or even their guinea pigs. So Charles usually attached himself to some kind-looking grown-up and walked inconspicuously at his heels until he was home.

On that day he happened to see Newman emerging from the railroad station, and knowing that Newman was going in the right direction, Charles walked in his shadow and felt safe.

"Perhaps I looked rather obtrusively at his protruding chin, for after we had walked some way the chin dropped and I saw a smile steal over the fixed mouth, a voice said tenderly, 'What is your name, little fellow?'

" 'Please, Mr. John Henry Newman,' I answered, 'I am Charles Marson and I am staying near you and I have got two guinea pigs and this little one which the man says is called Sugarplum.'

"We walked up to Edgbaston together and talked of guinea pigs and I observed with some wonder that he did not know much about them. After that a friendship was established: Father Newman would always laugh if he happened to see me take off my hat and bow profoundly to him. He always asked after Sugarplum and one joyful day he took my hand from the Five Ways to the 'Plough and Harrow' without speaking and when we parted he patted my head and said, 'Be a good boy and love God.' "

12

The Cloud Is Lifted

July 1, 1879

New Street Station, Birmingham. In this golden railway age
before the age of the automobile, a million exciting events
happen in railway stations. The best of them are built to make
a good background for excitement. They are vaulted like
enormous tunnels, full of hissing clouds of steam and echoing, piercing whistles; the clank of shunting coaches, and the
strange cries of porters. A railway train in the days of steam
arrived and departed more satisfyingly than any other means
of transport.

A first-class train is coming in from Rugby. There is a
red carpet on the platform, a great number of gentlemen in
top hats and frock coats looking dignified, small boys pushing
from the back of the crowd, a hovering of railway servants
in Great Western Railway caps and gold braid. A cloud of
steam coming around the bend, a clanking of oiled piston
rods, slow slurring of braked wheels, and the train draws in,
driblets of steam hissing from unexpected valves.

The group on the platform coagulates and pushes for-

ward. Then out of a first-class carriage step two priests, and
behind them, their careful arms making sure that he is safe,
emerges a bent figure, all nose and chin like Punch in the
cartoons. He smiles, somewhat nervously at first, for it is an
ordeal that he has never liked, facing a crowd, and he is more-
over very tired.

He is soon to learn how easy it is to be a great man. His
every smile will be taken as a treasure, his every kind word
saved up and repeated. For he is no longer John Henry Newman, but Cardinal Newman no less, with a red skullcap and a
silk cummerbund under his black coat, just returning from
Rome, where he has been dignified by the Pope.

The ceremony passes off quite well. His ring is kissed a
great number of times by half the priests of the diocese and
all the important laymen, and his Irish congregation stand in
the street and cheer him as he goes by. The priests of his own
Oratory are waiting for him at home.

A fine carriage, lent for the occasion by a lady of the
congregation, is waiting, pair of horses, coachman in livery,
and all. In steps the little old man, "doubled up like a shrimp,"
someone said, but beaming happily now. For it is good to be
loved and made welcome. Somehow on the road behind the
blinds of the carriage, they do a quick change. The black
clothes stuffed into a carpetbag, and out of another, not too
badly creased, the red-trimmed cassock and pink cape, red
biretta and skullcap—all the gaudy silken paraphernalia of a
prince of the Church.

"This is a strange turn-up. . . . It makes one giddy," was
John Henry's comment.

And it was strange—at one step to become a great man,
with regulations governing behavior. Ridiculous, some of it

seemed. A slice of his bedroom had had to be hastily boarded up to make a little chapel: new clothes, new robes, new vestments—his old friend the Duke of Norfolk was paying, thank goodness, because the bill was enormous. He would have to mind his p's and q's—no hearing confession in church, for instance, like any common-or-garden priest. It was satisfactory, and slyly amusing, to find oneself at the top of the Roman tree—"Bishops and Archbishops are nobodies."

The Birmingham Oratory now finds itself famous. Its fortunes have been gradually changing for the better for several years now, after a long period that seemed like stagnation, when there appeared to be no hope of any further development but the gradual dying of a handful of old men. It has begun to attract new recruits, though it is still not so grand or successful as the London Oratory, where they have just finished building their magnificent church.

Ambrose St. John is in his grave, but some of the old guard are still there, and whether they have in the past always agreed with him or not, today their hearts will lift with pride for the grand old man.

It begins to rain. The policeman on duty, holding back interested crowds, bolts inside to say in a hoarse whisper to the waiting community: "They're here sir," and bolts out again to stand at attention and salute.

Almost the whole of his trip to Rome, John Henry was ill with cold and cough and congestion of the lungs—imagine spending May in Rome and seeing not a thing, it had been very disappointing—and he was still weak. He looked taut and anxious as he went into the church, a newspaper reporter noticed, wondering no doubt whether he would get through the ritual safely. He had to walk under a grand canopy, there was incensing and prayers, and a long walk the length of the church, while the packed congregation knelt by rustling rows as he blessed them with a hand that trembled.

Then he had to sit in the sanctuary—a throne now, no less, no ordinary seat will do for a cardinal—while his priests came to kiss his ring. It was no mere formality—anyone could see that. They loved him as they congratulated him, felt with him the glory of the occasion. The clouds had lifted. That was how he had first announced the news to them all: "The cloud is lifted from me for ever."

They gathered around him to hear his address. The aged voice was not strong now at the best of times, and the newspaper reporter had to admit that he couldn't hear what the old man was saying, but watched instead the faces of those who could hear, and was moved to see how moved they were.

What in fact John Henry said, leaning his head on his hand with a gesture half of weariness, half of relief, was: "It is such happiness to come *home*." He spoke to them briefly and gave his blessing.

"He was wonderful to look upon as he sat fronting the congregation, his face as the face of an angel—the features that were so familiar to us refined and spiritualized by illness, and the delicate complexion and silver hair touched by the rose tints of his bright unaccustomed dress." This from one of the oldest members of the Oratory.

"He looks thin and weak from his recent illness, but this only adds to his magnificent appearance. I wish you could have heard the sermon. It made us all cry, more or less." This from the newest and most enthusiastic novice, perhaps the last (the first by now were of his grandfather's generation) to fall completely under the spell of John Henry Newman.

The ceremony ended and he left the church, very pleased with himself. He had got through the occasion very creditably. He was going to find out that it was not so difficult to be a Cardinal. There is a nice story of him trailing miserably off to his first public occasion (some eminent body wanted to present him with an address), dropping his gloves on the railway platform and generally looking so tired and feeble that it seemed a shame to let such an old man go all the way to London by himself. "It has all come too late," he said wearily. Met at the station that evening on his return, he bounced out of his carriage in fine form, looking ten years younger and announcing: "I did it all very well, very well indeed."

It seems fair that he should enjoy whatever glory came his way. Newman-like, he very nearly had a final stumble and almost missed his Cardinal's hat. In their last clash, Manning very nearly won.

There was a new Pope that year, 1879—Leo XIII succeeded Pius IX, and that meant the usual political upheavals throughout the Roman establishment. This Pope was thought to be more modern than the last, and at once people began to say: "He will honor John Henry Newman. The old guard is on the way out, and the greatest man of them all will at last get some recognition."

Such things are not easy. They are not even easy for a Pope. Leo XIII was reported to have said: "My Cardinal! It wasn't easy! They said he was too liberal. But I had determined to honor the Church in honoring Newman. I always had a cult for him. I am proud that I was allowed to honor such a man."

Having found out by some backstairs maneuvering that a request would be looked on favorably by the Pope, the Duke of Norfolk and some other friends decided to make a move. They went off to Westminster to lay their request before the Cardinal Archbishop, who of course would have to convey it to Rome for them. They could not bypass the proper channels.

One story has it that Manning was struck speechless. *Newman? A Cardinal?* Newman, whom he thought (and still thought to his dying day, never mind any number of red hats) to be a heretic? Not only did the thought paralyze him, but it was a bitter pill to have it come through the laity of England, that laity that he wanted kept firmly in its place.

However, in any political chess game, a cardinal may be outmaneuvered by a duke. Manning could not refuse a request from such a source, so he passed it on duly to Rome. Back came a note from Rome: would the Archbishop find out from Father Newman, or from his local bishop, whether such an offer would be acceptable?

What Newman felt was fully summed up in his words to his priests: "The cloud is lifted from me for ever!" But there was a slight difficulty in the way. He was seventy-nine and frail, though to be sure he had been a creaky door for a long time, convinced ever since he was in his twenties that he must die within a very few years. He could not possibly face going to Rome to live at his age. His Oratory needed him and he needed it. He could not live his last years in a new place among new faces.

But cardinals are the Pope's advisory council, and the rule is that unless they are bishops or archbishops, in which case they do not leave their see (like Manning, and Wiseman before him), they must go to Rome.

You can't really bargain with a Pope. It is not seemly to

answer, "Yes, your Holiness, I'll accept, *if.* . . ." so Newman wrote a careful letter, pleading old age and infirmity as a reason for not being able to live in Rome. At a first glance it might be taken for a refusal, but at a second it is quite obvious what is to be read between the lines. Newman sent this letter for forwarding to his bishop, Bishop Ullathorne, who had always been his friend, and the Bishop sent with it a covering letter. "I am thoroughly confident that nothing stands in the way of his grateful acceptance, except, what he tells me greatly distresses him, namely the having to leave the Oratory. . . ."

Manning forwarded Newman's refusal (not his letter) and did not forward Bishop Ullathorne's. Later, he talked about misunderstanding, but no misunderstanding was really possible. It seems simply as though he felt very strongly that Newman should not be a cardinal, and he did his best to save the Church from that doubtful honor.

One last word about Manning before he disappears from the story. Any book about Newman tends to use Manning as a convenient villain. He wasn't. But some of his opinions and actions have embarrassed people for so long that there is not even a proper biography of him. In this clash of antagonistic personalities, we shall not really see Newman quite straight until someone sees Manning quite straight, takes the trouble to follow the windings of that devious mind with the sympathy with which many people have followed the windings of Newman's devious mind.

Manning's scheme on this occasion did not work. News has a habit of leaking, and the next thing Newman knew, he was getting letters from all parts of England, including one from the Duke of Norfolk, asking why he had refused the red hat that had been offered, and regretting very much that he had done so. Norfolk, who had worked hard, was surprised and hurt.

These were difficult letters to answer. Newman said that he had not refused, because he had not been asked, which was true. He had not been asked directly from Rome. He could hardly state baldly that if the Pope invited him, and if the conditions were right, he would accept like a shot. For a few weeks it was all very muddled and delicate.

Ullathorne at least was in no doubt where the hitch had occurred. Though he himself was an old man and a bishop, Manning had him up and scolded him sharply, "as though I had been a boy," for daring to suggest Newman's name so warmly.

"You do not know Newman as I do." The Cardinal got quite excited. "He simply twists you round his little finger. He bamboozles you with his carefully selected words, and plays so subtly with his logic that your simplicity is taken in. You are no match for him!"

The Cardinal shouldn't have shown his hand quite so clearly. Ullathorne was an obstinate Yorkshireman, and he intended that Newman should have his red hat. Norfolk was on Newman's side too, and there was a great press of public opinion behind them, both Catholic and Protestant, for the story was out in the papers by this time. *Punch* welcomed it in verse:

A Cardinal's Hat! Fancy Newman in that!
For a crown o'er his grey temples spread;
'Tis the good and great head that would honour the hat,
Not the hat that would honour the head!

A little more maneuvering in dark places, a few more moves in the game of chess, a few more letters sent back and forth (all carefully copied now and sent by more than one route, so there could be no chance of anything being mislaid), and the thing was done.

"It is a wonderful providence," wrote Newman, "that even before my death that acquittal of men comes, which I knew would come some day or other, though not in my own life time."

On June 1, 1890, from the little town of Clare in Suffolk, the Reverend W. Wood sat down to write a letter with some misgivings. It was a letter he had meant to write for several months, but he had put it off from day to day; it seemed so strange for an Independent low church minister, from the manse attached to a brick chapel, to be writing to a prince of the Roman Church, obscured to his imagination by purple silk and clouds of incense. He did not know the proper way to begin or end the letter, much less what to put on the envelope.

In the end his sense of what was right overcame his doubts about what was proper, and he got his letter written and sent it off. And very glad he must have been to get what he wanted to say said. A few weeks later he opened his newspaper to find that John Henry, Cardinal Newman, aged eighty-nine stormy years, was dead. . . .

Dear Sir,
    I do not know the style in which I ought to address you but I am sure you will forgive any informality that springs from my not knowing the usages of your people; especially do I think you will be ready to overlook any

infringement of the outward laws of reverence due to your position when you know that I am writing this expressly to inform you as I think it is my duty to do, how much I owe to you.

The question of whether I should acknowledge my spiritual debt has been on my mind for some months. I have at last decided it in the way this letter shows.

And now I am at a loss to say what I feel towards you. Were it not for the perfect confidence established by your writings I should leave unsaid what I want so much to say. But that confidence begotten in me towards you leads me to endeavor to say quite simply what is in my heart.

About four years ago I came by the first three volumes of your *Parochial and Plain Sermons* and some time afterwards I bought an odd volume of selected sermons adapted to the seasons of the ecclesiastical year. These sermons, with the hymn "Lead Kindly Light" (so frequently sung by my congregation), are all that I have read of your writings. But how poorly should I say it if I attempted to put down how much I have received from those four volumes. Surely it is right that I should tell you, if I could, how my life has been changed, how my spirit has been fashioned, how the mind that was in Christ Jesus has been communicated to me by the reading of your sermons.

If I were to allow in myself a perfectly free and natural expression of feeling I should say with a feeling of grateful tears about my heart—"God bless you, Cardinal Newman, God bless you!"

Dates in the Life of John Henry Newman

1801   Born in London (January 21).

1808   Sent to school at Ealing.

1816   Ill at school. Experienced conversion.

1817   Took up residence at Trinity College, Oxford.

1822   Elected Fellow of Oriel College, Oxford.

1825   Ordained priest in Church of England.

1826   Appointed College Tutor at Oriel.

1830   Resigned tutorship at Oriel.

1833   Journeyed to Mediterranean and Sicily. On return journey wrote *Lead Kindly Light*. Wrote first *Tracts for the Times*.

1836   Consecration of Littlemore Church.

1841   Publication of *Tract 90*.

1843   Resigned as Vicar of St. Mary's, Oxford. Preached last sermon, "On the Parting of Friends," at Littlemore.

1845   Received into Roman Catholic Church (October 8).

1846   Went to Rome.

1847   Ordained priest in Roman Catholic Church.

1849   Foundation of Oratory in Birmingham.

1850   Foundation of London Oratory.

1864   Wrote *Apologia pro Vita Sua*.

1870   First Vatican Council convened.

1877   Elected first Honorary Fellow of Trinity College.

1879   Given Cardinal's hat in Rome by Pope Leo XIII.

1890   Died in Birmingham (August 11).

A Short Booklist

Esther Battiscombe: *John Keble* (1963)
Edward Bellasis: *Memorials of Mr. Serjeant Bellasis* (1923)
Louis Bouyer: *Newman, His Life and Spirituality* (1958)
Ronald Chapman: *Father Faber* (1961)
Geoffrey Faber: *Oxford Apostles* (1933)
Thomas Hughes: *Tom Brown at Oxford* (1861)
R. B. Martin: *The Dust of Combat* (Charles Kingsley) (1961)
Thomas Mozley: *Reminiscences of Oriel and Oxford* (1882)
Harriet Newman Mozley: *Family Adventures*
John Henry Newman: *Loss and Gain* (1848)
　　　　　　　　　　 Apologia pro Vita Sua (1864)
　　　　　　　　　　 Autobiographical Writings, edited by
　　　　　　　　　　　　 Henry Tristram (1956)
　　　　　　　　　　 Letters and Correspondence, edited by
　　　　　　　　　　　　 Anne Mozley (1890)
Sean O'Faolain: *Newman's Way* (1952)
E. E. Reynolds: *Three Cardinals* (1958)
Meriol Trevor: *Newman, The Pillar of the Cloud; Newman,*
　　　　　　　　 Light in Winter (1962)
Maisie Ward: *Young Mr. Newman* (1952)
Wilfrid Ward: *Life of John Henry, Cardinal Newman* (1912)

Index